The Leadership Pivot

Adapt, Innovate, Inspire

Olivia Savage

The Leadership Pivot: Adapt, Innovate, Inspire

ISBN: 979-8-9999006-2-3
Publisher: Deep End Publishing

Dedication

To my mentors, whose wisdom and guidance shaped my journey, and to my family, whose unwavering love and support have been my foundation. Thank you for believing in me and inspiring me every step of the way. To all the unsung heroes who lead with empathy, humility, and wisdom, this book is for you.

To the courageous leaders who embrace change, navigate uncertainty, and inspire others to thrive in the face of adversity. To those who understand that true leadership lies not in control, but in adaptability and resilience. To the countless individuals who, through their actions and perseverance, demonstrate the power of adaptive leadership every day. It is to them, the pioneers of progress, the champions of innovation, and the architects of a more flexible and responsive future, that this work is humbly dedicated.

Purpose of the Book

The purpose of this book is to equip leaders with the knowledge, skills, and tools necessary to navigate the complexities and uncertainties of today's ever-changing world. By exploring the principles of adaptive leadership, you will learn how to effectively manage change, inspire innovation, and lead with resilience. Whether you are a seasoned leader or just starting your leadership journey, this book aims to provide valuable insights and practical strategies to help you succeed.

Importance of Adaptive Leadership

In a world where change is the only constant, adaptive leadership has never been more important. Organizations face unprecedented challenges, from technological disruptions to global crises, and leaders must be able to pivot and adapt to these shifting landscapes. Adaptive leadership empowers leaders to be agile, responsive, and forward-thinking, enabling them to guide their teams through uncertainty and emerge stronger on the other side. By mastering adaptive leadership, you will not only enhance your own leadership capabilities but also contribute to the success and resilience of your organization.

Table of Contents

Preface

The world is changing at an unprecedented pace. Traditional leadership models, built on hierarchical structures and rigid plans, are increasingly inadequate in the face of rapid technological advancements, global interconnectedness, and unforeseen disruptions. This book, *"The Leadership Pivot,"* is born from the recognition of this critical need for a new paradigm in leadership – one that prioritizes adaptability, resilience, and continuous learning above all else.

For too long, leadership has been viewed as a position of control, a top-down approach focused on dictating strategies and enforcing compliance. In today's volatile landscape, however, effective leadership requires a fundamental shift—**a pivot**—towards a more agile and responsive approach. This book isn't simply a theoretical exploration of adaptive leadership; it is a practical guide designed to equip leaders at all levels with the tools and strategies they need to navigate complexity and uncertainty.

Through real-world case studies, actionable exercises, and insightful reflection prompts, you will develop the skills to build high-performing adaptive teams, foster a culture of continuous improvement, and lead with confidence and creativity even in the most challenging circumstances. Whether you're an emerging leader seeking to hone your skills, a seasoned executive looking to refine your approach, or an organizational development professional seeking to cultivate a culture of adaptability, this book offers a pathway to success in the ever-evolving world of leadership. It is a journey of continuous growth and adaptation, mirroring the very essence of the leadership style it advocates.

Introduction

The landscape of leadership is undergoing a seismic shift. Gone are the days when a rigid, top-down approach could effectively navigate the complexities of the business world. Today's leaders face unprecedented challenges: rapid technological advancements, globalization's complexities, and the constant threat of unforeseen disruptions. The traditional leadership models, often characterized by hierarchical structures and inflexible strategies, are proving inadequate in the face of this dynamic environment. *"The Leadership Pivot"* offers a timely and essential framework for navigating this new reality.

This book isn't just another leadership manual; it's a comprehensive guide to adaptive leadership – a style that embraces change, fosters resilience, and prioritizes continuous learning. It provides practical tools and strategies for leaders at all levels, from emerging managers to seasoned executives. We dive into the core principles of adaptability, examining how to build high-performing teams capable of responding swiftly and effectively to evolving circumstances.

You'll learn to cultivate a culture of innovation and experimentation, empowering your team to embrace change as an opportunity for growth. Furthermore, we explore the critical role of emotional intelligence in leading through challenging times, emphasizing the importance of empathy, clear communication, and building strong, trusting relationships. Through real-world case studies from diverse industries and engaging exercises, you'll gain a practical understanding of how to apply these principles in your own context. This is not a passive reading experience; it's an active journey of self-discovery and skill development.

Prepare to challenge your assumptions, refine your strategies, and ultimately, pivot your leadership style for success in today's dynamic world. This book will empower you to not just survive, but to thrive in the face of constant change, leading your organization towards a future of innovation and resilience.

Chapter 1: Understanding the Adaptive Leadership Landscape

Defining Adaptive Leadership in the 21st Century

The 21st-century business landscape is a maelstrom of constant change. Globalization, technological advancements, shifting consumer preferences, and unforeseen geopolitical events create an environment of unprecedented volatility and uncertainty. Traditional leadership models, often rooted in hierarchical structures, rigid processes, and command-and-control approaches, struggle to navigate this complexity. These models, effective in the more predictable environments of the past, often prove brittle and inadequate in the face of rapid and unpredictable change. They frequently stifle innovation, hinder adaptability, and ultimately lead to organizational stagnation or even failure. This chapter will dive into the evolving understanding of leadership, showcasing the limitations of traditional approaches and introducing the transformative power of adaptive leadership as a crucial response to the demands of our times.

Consider the rise and fall of companies like Blockbuster, a once-dominant video rental giant, that failed to adapt to the digital disruption brought about by Netflix's streaming service. Their rigid business model, resistant to change, led to their eventual demise, a stark contrast to Netflix's success built on its continuous adaptation and innovative strategies. Similarly, the automotive industry witnessed the swift rise of electric vehicle manufacturers, forcing established players to rapidly adapt their production lines and business strategies, or risk being left behind.

These examples illustrate the critical need for leaders who can not only manage existing operations but also anticipate, respond to, and proactively shape change. Adaptive leadership stands in sharp contrast to these traditional approaches. It's not simply about reacting to change; it's about proactively anticipating it, embracing uncertainty, and fostering an organizational culture that thrives on continuous learning and improvement. At its core, adaptive leadership emphasizes flexibility, resilience, and a commitment to continuous learning. It encourages experimentation, iterative improvement, and a willingness to embrace failure as an opportunity for growth. It recognizes that the future is inherently unpredictable and that the most effective leaders are those who can navigate ambiguity, make informed decisions with incomplete information, and guide their organizations through complex and rapidly evolving landscapes.

This contrasts sharply with traditional leadership paradigms that frequently prioritize control, predictability, and adherence to established plans. Traditional leaders often focus on maintaining the status quo, minimizing risk, and maximizing efficiency within existing structures. While these qualities are important, they alone are insufficient in today's volatile environment. Adaptive leadership, in contrast, demands a different skillset, one characterized by agility, creativity, and a willingness to step outside the comfort zone of established practices.

A key differentiator is the approach to problem-solving. Traditional models often rely on established procedures and pre-defined solutions, treating problems as deviations from the norm. Adaptive leadership, however, views challenges as opportunities for learning and growth. It encourages leaders and teams to explore various solutions, experiment with new approaches, and iteratively refine their strategies based on feedback and real-world results. This iterative, experimental approach is crucial for navigating the uncertainty inherent in today's business environment, allowing organizations to adapt and adjust their strategies as new information emerges and circumstances evolve.

Furthermore, adaptive leaders foster a culture of psychological safety. They create environments where individuals feel comfortable taking risks, expressing dissenting opinions, and learning from their mistakes. This contrasts starkly with traditional environments where fear of failure or retribution can stifle innovation and prevent necessary adjustments. In an adaptive leadership model, failure is not viewed as a personal shortcoming but rather as a valuable learning experience, providing insights that inform future strategies and decisions. This willingness to learn from setbacks is crucial in fostering resilience and adaptability within the organization.

The role of communication is also fundamentally different. Traditional leadership often relies on top-down communication, where information flows primarily from leaders to subordinates. Adaptive leadership, however, emphasizes open communication, feedback loops, and transparent information sharing. Leaders actively solicit input from all levels of the organization, fostering a sense of shared responsibility and collective ownership in navigating challenges and opportunities. This collaborative approach empowers team members, harnesses diverse perspectives, and enables the organization to respond more effectively to change.

The continuous learning aspect of adaptive leadership is particularly crucial. In a world characterized by exponential technological advancements and rapid shifts in market dynamics, maintaining a competitive edge requires a constant commitment to learning and development. Adaptive leaders recognize this and actively foster a culture of continuous learning within their organizations, providing opportunities for training, professional development, and knowledge sharing. They also emphasize the importance of embracing new technologies and incorporating them into their leadership strategies, ensuring that their organizations remain agile and responsive to evolving trends.

Adaptive leadership in the 21st century is a dynamic and evolving approach that prioritizes flexibility, resilience, and continuous learning over rigid structures and pre-defined solutions. It's about embracing uncertainty, fostering a culture of psychological safety, and empowering individuals to contribute to the organization's ability to adapt and thrive in the face of constant change. This approach demands a fundamental shift in leadership mindset and practices, moving away from controlling and managing towards empowering and guiding. The subsequent chapters will look deeper into the specific techniques and strategies that underpin this transformative leadership paradigm, providing practical tools and real-world examples to guide leaders on their journey towards achieving adaptive excellence. The successful adoption of adaptive leadership principles is not merely an advantage in today's volatile business environment; it is becoming a necessity for survival and sustained success.

Identifying the Challenges of Traditional Leadership Models

The inherent limitations of traditional leadership models become glaringly apparent when confronted with the complexities and uncertainties of the modern business environment. These models, often honed in eras of relative stability and predictable market conditions, frequently prove inadequate in navigating the volatile landscape of the

21st century. Their rigid structures, hierarchical decision-making processes, and resistance to change often act as significant impediments to organizational agility and adaptability. This section will explore these limitations in detail, illustrating how the inflexible nature of many traditional approaches directly contributes to organizational stagnation and even failure.

One of the most significant shortcomings of traditional leadership is its inherent resistance to change. Many organizations built upon hierarchical structures, with power concentrated at the top, are slow to adapt to evolving market demands. This centralized decision-making process often creates bureaucratic bottlenecks, hindering the organization's ability to respond quickly and decisively to new opportunities or emerging threats. Decisions are frequently delayed due to the need for multiple levels of approval, a process that can be painfully slow in the face of rapid market shifts. This rigidity often prevents the organization from pivoting strategically to capitalize on emerging trends or mitigating risks effectively.

Consider the example of the music industry's response to the rise of digital music distribution. Traditional record labels, accustomed to a model centered around physical media sales, were initially slow to adapt to the emergence of platforms like iTunes and later Spotify. Their hierarchical structures and ingrained processes made it challenging to embrace the new digital paradigm, leading to substantial losses in revenue and market share. In contrast, companies that embraced change early on, adapting their business models and distribution strategies to leverage digital platforms, thrived in the new environment. This contrast clearly demonstrates how resistance to change, a common characteristic of traditional leadership models, can lead to significant organizational challenges.

Another significant weakness of traditional models is the emphasis on control and predictability. These models often prioritize maintaining the status quo, minimizing risk, and maximizing efficiency within established frameworks. While these objectives are important, they can stifle innovation and creativity. The emphasis on adhering to strict procedures and pre-defined solutions often prevents the exploration of alternative approaches and the adoption of potentially disruptive technologies. Such an environment can stifle the entrepreneurial spirit, hindering the organization's capacity for innovation and adaptability.

A clear example of this can be seen in the automotive industry's initial response to the emergence of electric vehicles. Established automakers, initially focused on internal combustion engine technology and well-established production lines, were slow to adapt to the disruption caused by Tesla and other electric vehicle manufacturers. Their adherence to existing processes and a reluctance to embrace new technologies led to a significant loss of market share, highlighting the dangers of prioritizing control and predictability over innovation and adaptability. In contrast, organizations that actively embraced the transition to electric vehicles, adapting their production lines and investing in new technologies, maintained their competitiveness and even gained market share.

Hierarchical decision-making, another defining characteristic of many traditional leadership models, also presents considerable limitations. The concentration of power at the top often restricts the flow of information and limits the involvement of employees at lower levels in the decision-making process. This can lead to a disconnect between leadership and the workforce, with valuable insights and perspectives from front-line employees often being overlooked. Moreover, the top-down approach often creates a climate of fear and inhibition, reducing creativity and innovation. This lack of employee engagement can significantly impede the organization's ability to respond effectively to change, as crucial insights and valuable feedback remain untapped.

The focus on efficiency and optimization within existing structures, while important for operational effectiveness, can also become a limiting factor in the face of significant change. Traditional leadership models often prioritize incremental improvements within the confines of established processes, rather than fundamental transformations in response to disruptive forces. This approach is often insufficient when dealing with major market shifts or technological advancements that demand radical changes in strategy and operations. Organizations clinging to optimizing existing processes, without addressing the core need for transformation, risk becoming obsolete. The inability to envision and execute a fundamental shift in strategy can severely hamper the organization's long-term survival and success.

Furthermore, traditional leadership models frequently lack a culture of psychological safety. In many traditional organizations, employees may hesitate to challenge established norms or offer alternative solutions due to a fear of retribution or negative consequences. This stifles creativity, limits innovation, and prevents the organization from adapting effectively to new circumstances. This lack of psychological safety can significantly hinder the organization's capacity to learn from mistakes, embrace experimentation, and iterate effectively towards better solutions. A culture that penalizes failure rather than embracing it as a learning opportunity inherently limits the organization's ability to adapt and grow.

The consequences of these limitations are far-reaching. Organizations relying on traditional leadership models often find themselves ill-equipped to respond to unforeseen events, disruptive technologies, and rapidly shifting market dynamics. They struggle to innovate, adapt, and ultimately, thrive in the dynamic environment of the 21st century. The examples cited – from the music industry's response to digital distribution to the automotive industry's reaction to electric vehicles – highlight the critical need for a more flexible, adaptive leadership approach. The limitations of traditional models are not merely theoretical; they are demonstrably evident in the struggles of many organizations to survive and prosper in today's turbulent and ever-changing world. The case for a paradigm shift towards adaptive leadership is undeniable and compelling.

The next sections will explore the principles and practices of adaptive leadership, offering a roadmap for organizations seeking to navigate the complexities and uncertainties of the modern business landscape with agility, resilience, and success.

The Importance of Continuous Learning and Feedback Loops

The transition from traditional leadership paradigms to adaptive leadership necessitates a fundamental shift in organizational culture, one that prioritizes continuous learning and the establishment of robust feedback loops. Without these elements, any attempt at fostering adaptability remains superficial and ultimately ineffective. Adaptive leadership isn't simply about reacting to change; it's about proactively anticipating shifts in the market, embracing uncertainty, and continuously refining strategies based on real-time feedback and ongoing learning. This requires a concerted effort to cultivate a culture where learning is not a peripheral activity but the very lifeblood of the organization.

One of the most effective strategies for fostering a culture of continuous learning is to invest heavily in employee training and development programs. These programs should go beyond the traditional focus on technical skills, encompassing broader areas like critical thinking, problem-solving, and adaptability. The aim is to equip employees with the cognitive tools and mental models necessary to navigate ambiguity and uncertainty effectively. This includes training in areas such as scenario planning, strategic foresight, and decision-making under pressure.

These programs should be tailored to the specific needs of the organization and its employees, with a focus on practical application and real-world relevance. Regular assessments and evaluations should be conducted to ensure the programs are achieving their objectives and to identify areas for improvement. The organization should also invest in developing internal resources and expertise, creating a pool of knowledge and experience that can be readily accessed by all employees.

Organizations must actively cultivate a robust mentoring culture. Experienced leaders should be paired with rising stars, providing guidance, support, and valuable insights based on their own experiences. This mentoring relationship should not be a one-way street; rather, it should involve reciprocal learning, with both the mentor and the mentee exchanging knowledge and perspectives. Mentoring programs can serve as a powerful mechanism for disseminating best practices, transferring tacit knowledge, and promoting a culture of continuous learning. The organization should establish a structured framework for mentorship, including clear guidelines for pairing mentors and mentees, defining roles and responsibilities, and providing regular feedback on program effectiveness. Successful mentorship programs often incorporate regular check-ins, structured activities, and clear objectives, ensuring that both mentor and mentee are actively engaged in the learning process.

Beyond formal training and mentorship, the effective use of feedback mechanisms is crucial for continuous learning and improvement. This involves establishing systems for gathering feedback from various sources – employees at all levels, customers, suppliers, and even competitors. The feedback process should be designed to be transparent, constructive, and actionable. This means creating a safe space where individuals feel comfortable sharing their perspectives without fear of reprisal or negative consequences. Organizations should utilize a variety of methods for collecting feedback, such as employee surveys, focus groups, 360-degree feedback systems, and regular performance reviews. The data gathered should be analyzed thoroughly to identify recurring themes, patterns, and areas for improvement. This data-driven approach ensures that improvements are not merely based on intuition or anecdotal evidence, but on a solid foundation of objective information.

Crucially, adaptive organizations don't simply collect feedback; they actively use it to improve processes, strategies, and decision-making. This requires a commitment to transparency and accountability, with leadership actively demonstrating a willingness to act on feedback received. Feedback should be integrated into the organization's decision-making processes, with leaders demonstrating a willingness to adapt plans and strategies based on new information and insights. This might include adjusting project timelines, revising strategies, or even abandoning entirely projects that are no longer aligned with organizational goals or market realities. The ability to rapidly course-correct based on feedback is a hallmark of adaptive organizations.

A critical component of continuous learning within adaptive organizations is the embrace of failure as a learning opportunity. In many traditional organizations, failure is viewed as a taboo subject, something to be avoided at all costs. This fear of failure often stifles innovation and prevents organizations from taking calculated risks necessary for growth and progress. In contrast, adaptive organizations recognize that failure is an inevitable part of the learning process. Instead of punishing failure, these organizations actively encourage experimentation, learning from mistakes, and iterating towards better solutions. They create a culture of psychological safety, where employees feel comfortable taking risks and admitting mistakes without fear of reprisal.

This shift in perspective necessitates a change in mindset from a fixed mindset to a growth mindset. A fixed mindset assumes that abilities and intelligence are innate and unchangeable, leading to a reluctance to embrace challenges and a fear of failure. In contrast, a growth mindset views abilities and intelligence as malleable and improvable through effort and learning. This mindset fosters a culture of continuous improvement, resilience, and adaptability.

Organizations can promote a growth mindset through various initiatives, such as providing ongoing training and development opportunities, encouraging employees to embrace challenges, celebrating learning from mistakes, and providing constructive feedback that focuses on improvement rather than criticism. Leadership plays a crucial role in modeling this growth mindset, openly acknowledging their own learning journey and encouraging risk-taking and experimentation within the organization.

Consider the example of Netflix. Their success is significantly attributed to their continuous learning culture. They regularly collect data on viewing habits, user preferences, and content performance. This data informs their content creation strategies, algorithm development, and even their overall business model. They're not afraid to experiment with new formats, genres, and distribution methods, and they learn from both successes and failures, constantly iterating and adapting their approach based on the feedback they receive.

Similarly, companies like Google actively cultivate a culture of experimentation, encouraging employees to devote a portion of their time to exploring new ideas and projects, even if they are outside their core business. This allows for innovation and the discovery of new opportunities, while providing a wealth of learning experiences for employees. These organizations prioritize continuous learning and feedback not as an add-on, but as an integral part of their core operational strategy.

The importance of continuous learning and feedback loops cannot be overstated in the context of adaptive leadership. It's not merely a best practice; it's a fundamental necessity for navigating the complexities and uncertainties of the modern business landscape. By fostering a culture that prioritizes learning, experimentation, and the active use of feedback, organizations can enhance their agility, resilience, and capacity for continuous improvement, ultimately ensuring their long-term success and sustainability. The journey towards becoming a truly adaptive organization is a continuous one, requiring a sustained commitment to learning and improvement at all levels of the organization.

However, the rewards of this commitment are substantial, leading to greater organizational effectiveness, increased innovation, and enhanced adaptability in the face of constant change. Investing in these processes is not an expense; it's an investment in the future of the organization, ensuring its continued relevance and success in an increasingly dynamic and uncertain world.

Building Resilience and Fostering Psychological Safety

Building individual resilience is paramount in navigating the complexities of adaptive leadership. Resilience isn't merely the ability to bounce back from adversity; it's a proactive process of developing the mental, emotional, and physical capacity to withstand and adapt to challenges. This involves cultivating a growth mindset, where setbacks are viewed not as failures, but as opportunities for learning and growth. Individuals with a growth mindset are more likely to persist in the face of adversity, learn from their mistakes, and emerge stronger from challenging experiences.

One key component of building individual resilience is emotional intelligence. This involves understanding and managing one's own emotions, as well as recognizing and responding effectively to the emotions of others.

Individuals with high emotional intelligence are better able to navigate interpersonal conflicts, build strong relationships, and manage stress effectively. They are also more adept at empathizing with others, fostering a sense of trust and collaboration within the team. Developing emotional intelligence requires self-awareness, self-regulation, motivation, empathy, and social skills. This can be achieved through various means, including mindfulness practices, emotional regulation techniques, and active listening skills training. Organizations can support this by providing resources such as workshops, coaching, or mentoring programs focused on emotional intelligence development.

Stress management is another critical aspect of building individual resilience. The demands of adaptive leadership often involve navigating ambiguity, uncertainty, and high-pressure situations. Prolonged exposure to stress can lead to burnout, decreased productivity, and impaired decision-making. Effective stress management techniques are essential for maintaining well-being and performance. These techniques include mindfulness meditation, regular exercise, sufficient sleep, a healthy diet, and engaging in activities that promote relaxation and rejuvenation. Organizations can support employees' stress management efforts by providing resources such as wellness programs, employee assistance programs, and flexible work arrangements. Promoting work-life balance is crucial, allowing employees time to recharge and avoid burnout. Creating a culture that prioritizes employee well-being demonstrates a commitment to their success and overall mental health. This is a critical factor in cultivating a resilient workforce capable of handling the pressures inherent in adaptive leadership.

Beyond individual resilience, fostering psychological safety within the organization is crucial. Psychological safety is a shared belief that the team is safe for interpersonal risk-taking. In an environment of psychological safety, individuals feel comfortable expressing their opinions, admitting mistakes, and asking for help without fear of negative consequences. This is essential for creating a culture of continuous learning, where individuals feel empowered to experiment, innovate, and learn from their failures. It's important to distinguish between psychological safety and complacency – psychological safety encourages risk-taking, but it also fosters responsible behavior and accountability. Creating psychological safety requires a deliberate and sustained effort from leadership. Leaders must model vulnerability by openly sharing their own mistakes and challenges. This sets a tone of transparency and openness, encouraging others to do the same. Leaders should actively listen to employees' concerns, acknowledging their perspectives and validating their feelings. They should create opportunities for open communication, providing platforms for employees to share their ideas and feedback without fear of retribution. This might involve regular team meetings, anonymous feedback mechanisms, or informal channels for communication. Constructive feedback should always focus on improvement rather than criticism, providing guidance and support for growth rather than judgment and blame.

A key element in fostering psychological safety is establishing clear expectations and guidelines for behavior. This isn't about creating a rigid structure, but rather about establishing shared values and norms that promote respect, collaboration, and inclusiveness. This might involve developing a team charter that outlines the team's values, communication protocols, and conflict resolution strategies. The team charter should be collaboratively developed, ensuring buy-in and ownership from all team members. Regular review and refinement of the charter ensures it remains relevant and responsive to the evolving needs of the team.

High-performing organizations that prioritize psychological safety often employ several key strategies. They encourage open dialogue and feedback, creating forums where dissenting opinions are welcomed and valued. They celebrate failures as learning opportunities, fostering a culture of experimentation and innovation where taking risks is encouraged. They provide employees with autonomy and control over their work, empowering them to make decisions and take ownership of their projects. They offer ongoing training and development opportunities, supporting employees in developing the skills and competencies they need to succeed. They provide regular recognition and appreciation for employees' contributions, creating a sense of belonging and purpose within the team. This creates a positive feedback loop where employees feel valued, motivated, and empowered to contribute their best work.

The cultivation of psychological safety is a continuous process, requiring sustained commitment from leadership and all team members. It's not a one-time fix, but rather an ongoing journey of creating and reinforcing a culture where individuals feel safe, respected, and valued. This investment in psychological safety yields significant returns, fostering higher levels of creativity, innovation, collaboration, and overall organizational effectiveness. It builds a resilient and high-performing team, capable of navigating the complexities and uncertainties of the modern business environment.

Consider the example of Google's Project Aristotle, a research initiative that sought to identify the key characteristics of high-performing teams. Their research revealed that psychological safety was the single most important factor in team success. Teams with high levels of psychological safety were more likely to be innovative, productive, and engaged. This underscores the critical importance of fostering psychological safety in creating high-performing teams capable of thriving in the dynamic environment of adaptive leadership. Similarly, many other successful companies, such as Southwest Airlines and SAS Institute, have prioritized creating cultures of psychological safety and trust, contributing significantly to their sustained success and high levels of employee engagement and retention.

Building resilience and fostering psychological safety are intertwined and indispensable components of adaptive leadership. By cultivating individual resilience through emotional intelligence, stress management, and a growth mindset, and by creating an organizational culture of psychological safety, leaders can empower their teams to navigate change, embrace challenges, and achieve extraordinary results. This is not merely about surviving change, but about thriving in it, adapting and evolving to meet the ever-shifting demands of the modern business landscape. The investment in these areas is not just an expense, but a strategic imperative for long-term organizational success and sustainability in an era defined by continuous change and disruption. The journey towards building resilience and psychological safety is an ongoing process of learning, adaptation, and continuous improvement. The rewards, however, are significant, creating a high performing, engaged, and resilient workforce ready to face any challenge.

Assessing Your Current Leadership Style and Identifying Areas for Improvement

Assessing your leadership style is a crucial first step toward becoming a truly adaptive leader. Understanding your strengths and weaknesses allows you to focus your development efforts effectively, maximizing your impact and effectiveness. This self-assessment isn't about judgment; it's about honest introspection, a critical element of continuous learning and improvement. The goal is to identify areas for growth, enabling you to become a more flexible, resilient, and ultimately, more successful leader.

Begin by reflecting on your typical responses to change. Do you embrace new challenges with enthusiasm, viewing them as opportunities for growth? Or do you tend to resist change, clinging to familiar processes and routines? Honest reflection on past experiences will illuminate your natural inclination. Consider specific instances where your team or organization faced significant changes. How did you respond? Did you actively participate in shaping the change, or did you primarily react to it? Did you empower your team to adapt or did you primarily focus on controlling outcomes?

Consider your approach to decision-making. Are you decisive and willing to make quick judgments based on limited information, or do you prefer to gather exhaustive data before taking action? Adaptive leadership requires a balance. While thorough analysis is important, excessive deliberation can lead to missed opportunities in dynamic environments. The ability to make informed decisions quickly, even with incomplete information, is a hallmark of effective adaptive leaders.

Think about your communication style. Do you communicate openly and honestly, encouraging feedback and diverse perspectives? Or do you tend to control the flow of information, preferring to direct rather than collaborate? Effective communication is the cornerstone of any successful leadership approach, and adaptive leadership is no exception. Open communication fosters collaboration, enabling teams to navigate complexities and overcome challenges collectively.

Examine your feedback mechanisms. How do you provide feedback to your team members? Is it constructive and supportive, focusing on growth and improvement? Or is it primarily critical and judgmental? The way you deliver feedback significantly impacts team morale, engagement, and overall performance. Constructive feedback promotes learning, while harsh criticism can hinder growth and erode trust. Adaptive leadership fosters a culture of continuous learning, where mistakes are seen as opportunities for growth, not grounds for reprimand. This necessitates a shift in feedback delivery to focus on improvement rather than punishment.

Reflect on your ability to delegate effectively. Do you trust your team members to take ownership of tasks and make decisions independently? Or do you micromanage, retaining tight control over every aspect of the work? Delegation is a critical skill for any leader, especially in adaptive leadership. It frees up your time to focus on strategic priorities, empowers team members, and fosters a culture of trust and collaboration. Effective delegation also necessitates providing the necessary support and resources to your team, along with clear expectations and guidelines.

Consider your approach to conflict resolution. How do you handle disagreements within your team? Do you actively engage in conflict resolution, seeking collaborative solutions? Or do you avoid conflict, hoping it will resolve itself? Conflict is inevitable in any team, and adaptive leadership necessitates a proactive approach to its resolution. Effective conflict resolution strengthens relationships and enhances collaboration, resulting in more effective problem-solving and improved outcomes.

Now let's investigate identifying personal biases that might hinder your adaptability. We all hold implicit biases – unconscious beliefs and attitudes that can affect our decisions and actions without our awareness. These biases, if left unchecked, can significantly limit your capacity to adapt and lead effectively. For example, confirmation bias – the tendency to seek out information that confirms pre-existing beliefs and ignore contradictory evidence – can severely hinder your ability to respond effectively to new information and unexpected challenges. Similarly, anchoring bias – relying too heavily on the first piece of information received– can lead to poor decision-making in dynamic situations.

To identify your personal biases, consider seeking external feedback. Ask trusted colleagues, mentors, or even direct reports for honest assessments of your strengths and weaknesses. Their perspectives can offer valuable insights you might miss in self-reflection. Engage in activities that encourage self-reflection and introspection. Journaling, mindfulness practices, and regular self-assessment exercises can help you become more aware of your biases and their impact on your leadership style. Self-awareness is a critical component of adaptive leadership, allowing you to recognize and address your blind spots, ultimately becoming a more effective and empathetic leader.

Improving your emotional intelligence is key to enhancing your adaptability. Emotional intelligence encompasses your ability to understand and manage your own emotions, as well as recognize and respond effectively to the emotions of others. It's about being self-aware, empathetic, and skilled in managing interpersonal relationships. The development of emotional intelligence is a continuous process; it requires self-reflection, active listening, and a commitment to improving your interpersonal skills. There are several resources available to assist in this development, including workshops, coaching programs, and online courses that provide structured learning and practical exercises to enhance your emotional intelligence. These programs can help you develop skills in areas such as active listening, conflict resolution, and empathy, contributing significantly to your overall leadership effectiveness.

To further support your self-assessment, consider utilizing established leadership assessment tools. Numerous reputable assessments, such as the Myers-Briggs Type Indicator (MBTI), the Emotional Quotient Inventory (EQ-i), and various 360-degree feedback tools, offer structured frameworks to analyze your leadership style and pinpoint areas for improvement. These tools provide valuable insights into your strengths and weaknesses, offering a more comprehensive and objective assessment of your leadership capabilities. Remember, the goal of these assessments isn't self-criticism but rather a clear understanding of your leadership style to facilitate personal and professional growth.

The process of assessing your leadership style and identifying areas for improvement is ongoing. It's not a one-time event, but a continuous journey of self-reflection, learning, and adaptation. Regular self-assessment, combined with seeking feedback from others, is essential to ensure your leadership style remains aligned with the demands of a dynamic environment. Embrace this process as an opportunity for growth, and you will become a more adaptable, resilient, and impactful leader, navigating the complexities of today's world with confidence and expertise.

Adaptive leadership isn't about achieving perfection; it's about continuous learning, improvement, and the capacity to navigate change effectively, consistently adjusting your approach as the landscape shifts. By embracing this mindset, you not only strengthen your own leadership but also cultivate a more adaptable and resilient organization.

Chapter 2: Developing Strategic Agility

Foresight and Strategic Planning in Uncertain Times

Developing robust foresight and strategic planning capabilities is paramount for navigating the turbulent waters of today's business landscape. The traditional, linear approach to strategic planning, predicated on stable environments and predictable futures, is woefully inadequate in the face of accelerating technological advancements, geopolitical shifts, and unpredictable economic cycles. To thrive, organizations must cultivate a proactive, adaptive approach that anticipates change, embraces uncertainty, and leverages it as a source of opportunity rather than a threat. This requires a fundamental shift in mindset, moving away from rigid, long-term plans towards a more agile and iterative approach. Instead of clinging to a predetermined roadmap, adaptive organizations view their strategies as dynamic instruments, constantly calibrated and refined in response to new information and emerging trends. This isn't about abandoning long-term vision; rather, it's about developing the capacity to pursue that vision through flexible, iterative strategies.

One of the most effective tools for developing foresight in uncertain times is scenario planning. Scenario planning involves constructing multiple plausible narratives about the future, each reflecting different potential combinations of key uncertainties. Instead of predicting a single future, scenario planning helps organizations prepare for a range of possibilities, enhancing their resilience and adaptability. This process begins with identifying key uncertainties – factors that are both important and uncertain. These could include technological breakthroughs, shifts in consumer preferences, regulatory changes, or geopolitical events. Once identified, these uncertainties are used to develop several distinct scenarios, each outlining a different potential future based on different combinations of these uncertainties.

For example, a consumer goods company might consider scenarios like:

Scenario 1 (Optimistic): Strong economic growth, increasing consumer confidence, and successful product innovation.

Scenario 2 (Pessimistic): Economic recession, reduced consumer spending, and increased competition.

Scenario 3 (Disruptive): A significant technological advancement disrupts the market, creating new opportunities and threats.

By developing detailed narratives for each scenario, including potential market impact, competitive responses, and internal implications, the company can proactively identify potential vulnerabilities and develop contingency plans. This allows them to make informed decisions, allocate resources strategically, and adapt quickly as the future unfolds.

Complementing scenario planning is environmental scanning, a systematic process of monitoring and analyzing external factors that could impact the organization. This involves gathering information from a wide range of sources, including industry reports, news articles, social media,
competitor analysis, and regulatory filings. The goal is to identify emerging trends, potential disruptions, and opportunities before they significantly impact the organization. This process should not be confined to a single department but should involve cross-functional collaboration, ensuring a comprehensive and holistic view of the external environment.

Effective environmental scanning requires the development of a structured process. This may include establishing regular monitoring schedules, utilizing sophisticated data analytics tools, and maintaining a network of external contacts to provide insights and early warnings. For example, a financial institution might utilize environmental scanning to monitor macroeconomic trends, geopolitical risks, and regulatory changes. By constantly monitoring these factors, the institution can anticipate potential financial shocks, adjust its investment strategies, and mitigate risk exposure. This proactive approach allows the organization to maintain stability and profitability, even amidst significant market volatility.

However, foresight is not simply about predicting the future; it's about shaping it. This involves actively engaging with stakeholders, influencing trends, and developing strategies that proactively address potential challenges. For instance, a technology company might participate in industry consortia, engage in public policy debates, and invest in research and development to influence the trajectory of technological advancements. This proactive approach positions the company not merely as a respondent to change but as a shaper of it.

Incorporating flexibility into strategic plans is crucial in uncertain environments. Traditional strategic planning often involves rigid, long-term plans that are difficult to adapt once circumstances change. However, in dynamic environments, it's essential to build flexibility into the planning process. This may involve developing modular strategies, which can be easily adapted or reconfigured to suit different circumstances. It also involves creating contingency plans that outline alternative courses of action if certain events occur. For example, a manufacturing company might develop modular production lines that can be easily reconfigured to produce different products, allowing them to quickly respond to changes in consumer demand.

Effective strategic planning in uncertain times involves establishing a strong organizational culture that values learning, experimentation, and adaptability. This involves fostering a culture of continuous learning, where employees are encouraged to embrace new ideas and challenge existing assumptions. It also involves building strong communication channels, empowering employees to make decisions, and creating a climate of trust and psychological safety. In such an environment, employees are more likely to identify potential problems, propose solutions, and adapt quickly to changing circumstances.

The process of strategic forecasting involves the use of various analytical techniques to anticipate future trends. This may include quantitative methods like forecasting models, econometric analyses, and time series analysis, as well as qualitative approaches like expert surveys, Delphi studies, and scenario planning. The choice of method depends on the specific context, data availability, and level of uncertainty. Crucially, these methods should not be used in isolation but should be integrated into a broader framework that includes qualitative insights and strategic considerations.

Numerous successful companies exemplify this adaptive strategic planning approach. For example, Netflix's continuous innovation and ability to adapt to changing consumer preferences and technological advancements have solidified its position as a global streaming leader. Their agile approach to content creation, distribution, and algorithm optimization reflects their commitment to dynamic strategic planning. Similarly, Amazon's consistent evolution, pivoting from online bookstore to a dominant force in e-commerce, cloud computing, and numerous other sectors, showcases the power of adaptive strategic thinking. Their relentless focus on customer needs and rapid experimentation demonstrate their unwavering commitment to iteratively adjusting their strategy.

Ultimately, developing foresight and engaging in effective strategic planning requires a holistic approach that integrates multiple perspectives, analytical tools, and organizational capabilities. It's not about predicting the future with certainty, but about enhancing the organization's ability to anticipate, adapt, and thrive in the face of unpredictable changes. By cultivating a culture of adaptability, embracing new technologies, and developing flexible strategies, organizations can transform uncertainty from a threat into an opportunity for innovation and growth. The ability to learn, unlearn, and relearn is no longer a luxury but a fundamental requirement for survival and success.

Embracing Change and Managing Disruption

Embracing change isn't merely about reacting to unforeseen circumstances; it's about proactively shaping the organization's trajectory to navigate inevitable disruptions effectively. This requires a fundamental shift in mindset, moving from a reactive stance to a proactive one, anticipating challenges and opportunities before they materialize. Understanding the diverse nature of change is the first crucial step. Change can be incremental, occurring gradually over time, or it can be disruptive, characterized by sudden and significant shifts. Incremental change, such as a gradual shift in consumer preferences, allows for a more measured response. Disruptive change, like the advent of a revolutionary technology, demands a rapid and decisive reaction.

Developing a robust change management strategy is paramount. This strategy should encompass several key components. First, it necessitates a clear articulation of the need for change. This involves transparently communicating the reasons behind the change, its potential impact on the organization, and the intended outcomes. Ambiguity breeds uncertainty and resistance, so clarity is crucial. Furthermore, the strategy must establish a strong leadership team dedicated to championing the change initiative. These leaders must not only articulate the vision but also actively model the desired behaviors and attitudes. This demonstrates commitment and builds confidence amongst employees.

A comprehensive change management strategy also requires a detailed plan with clearly defined goals, timelines, and resources. This involves breaking down the change into manageable steps, setting measurable milestones, and allocating the necessary resources – both human and financial – to support the implementation. This detailed planning process minimizes unforeseen complications and allows for efficient tracking of progress. Equally important is the development of strong communication channels to keep everyone informed and engaged throughout the change process. Regular updates, open forums, and feedback mechanisms ensure transparency and build trust.

Managing resistance to change is an inevitable aspect of any transformation. Resistance stems from various sources, including fear of the unknown, loss of control, and lack of understanding. Addressing this resistance effectively involves active listening, addressing concerns, and fostering a collaborative environment. Participatory decision-making, where employees are involved in the design and implementation of the change, significantly reduces resistance by giving them a sense of ownership. Training and development programs can help employees acquire new skills and knowledge, reducing anxiety about the future. Effective communication remains central, reassuring employees and addressing their concerns directly.

Case studies provide valuable insights into navigating disruptive events. The COVID-19 pandemic serves as a powerful example. Businesses that swiftly adapted their operations, leveraging digital technologies and remote work strategies, weathered the storm more successfully.

Conversely, organizations that clung to traditional models faced significant challenges. The rapid transition to remote work, accelerated by the pandemic, compelled many companies to invest heavily in digital infrastructure and communication tools. This investment proved essential for maintaining operational continuity and employee engagement. Those companies that invested proactively in digital transformation prior to the pandemic were better equipped to adapt.

Similarly, the rise of e-commerce significantly disrupted traditional brick-and-mortar retail. Companies that failed to adapt to the shift to online shopping faced declining sales and eventual closure. Successful retailers, however, embraced the change by establishing robust e-commerce platforms, optimizing their online presence, and integrating online and offline channels. Many retailers successfully integrated omnichannel strategies, allowing customers to seamlessly browse and purchase products across various platforms. This illustrates how successfully adapting to disruptive forces requires a willingness to innovate and transform business models.

Technological breakthroughs frequently disrupt industries, creating both opportunities and threats. The advent of artificial intelligence (AI) is a prime example. Companies that successfully integrate AI into their operations gain a competitive edge by enhancing efficiency, productivity, and decision-making. However, those that fail to adapt risk becoming obsolete. Consider companies in the manufacturing sector. The integration of robotic process automation (RPA) has transformed many manufacturing processes, leading to increased efficiency and lower production costs. Those companies slow to embrace RPA are facing heightened competition.

Successfully managing disruptive events relies heavily on a strong organizational culture. This culture must embrace flexibility, continuous learning, and adaptability. A culture of innovation encourages experimentation and risk-taking, allowing companies to explore new ideas and develop innovative solutions. A culture that values continuous learning promotes employee development and enables organizations to adapt swiftly to evolving circumstances. This involves actively seeking new knowledge, providing opportunities for skill development, and fostering an environment where employees feel comfortable sharing their ideas.

Beyond fostering a culture of adaptability, effective leadership is crucial for navigating change. Leaders must be decisive, communicative, and transparent throughout the change process. They need to clearly articulate the vision and effectively manage expectations. Moreover, leaders must build trust and confidence within the team, motivating employees and inspiring them to embrace the change. This leadership approach involves actively listening to employee concerns, providing support, and celebrating successes.

Embracing change and managing disruption is not a passive process but an active, strategic initiative. It requires a clear understanding of the nature of change, the development of robust change management strategies, and the ability to manage resistance effectively. Learning from real-world examples, such as the responses to the COVID-19 pandemic and the rise of e-commerce, provides valuable insights. Ultimately, a culture of adaptability, continuous learning, and effective leadership are essential for navigating the uncertainties and harnessing the opportunities that disruption presents, transforming challenges into a springboard for innovation and growth. The companies that thrive in this dynamic environment are those that prioritize adaptability, not as a reaction to change, but as a core competency for sustained success.

Decision Making Frameworks for Uncertain Environments

The ability to make sound judgments in ambiguous situations is paramount for organizations striving for strategic agility. Traditional decision-making models often falter when faced with incomplete information, rapidly evolving circumstances, and high levels of uncertainty hallmarks of today's dynamic business landscape. This section explores decision-making frameworks specifically designed to thrive in such unpredictable environments. These frameworks are not mutually exclusive; instead, they often complement each other, providing a multifaceted approach to navigating complexity.

One powerful approach is evidence-based decision-making (EBDM). EBDM prioritizes the systematic use of the best available evidence to inform decisions. This means moving beyond intuition and gut feelings, relying instead on data, research, and analysis to guide choices. The process starts with clearly defining the problem or opportunity at hand. This clarity forms the foundation for targeted research, allowing the organization to identify and evaluate relevant information. The sources of this evidence can be diverse, including internal data (sales figures, customer feedback, operational metrics), external data (market research, industry reports, competitor analysis), and expert opinion.

Crucially, EBDM is not simply about gathering data; it's about critically evaluating its quality, reliability, and relevance. This requires a thorough understanding of the limitations of any data source. For example, relying solely on customer surveys might overlook the perspectives of customers who don't participate in such surveys. Similarly, historical data may not accurately predict future trends in rapidly evolving markets. By critically evaluating the data and identifying potential biases, decision-makers can avoid making flawed judgments based on incomplete or misleading information. Robust data analysis and statistical modeling help to uncover underlying trends and patterns, improving the accuracy of predictions and forecasts. The results of this analysis should be clearly communicated to stakeholders, ensuring transparency and buy-in for the decisions made.

Scenario planning offers another valuable tool for navigating uncertain environments. Unlike traditional forecasting methods, which typically focus on a single, most-likely outcome, scenario planning explores a range of possible futures. This involves identifying key drivers of uncertainty– factors that could significantly impact the organization's future – and developing plausible scenarios based on different combinations of these drivers. For instance, a technology company might develop scenarios based on various levels of market adoption for its new product, considering factors such as competitor actions, regulatory changes, and economic conditions. Each scenario would outline a distinct future state and the implications for the organization's strategy and operations.

The benefit of scenario planning is not necessarily to predict the future with precision, but rather to enhance preparedness for a wider range of possibilities. By actively considering various potential outcomes, the organization can develop contingency plans and build resilience. This proactive approach allows for more effective adaptation when unforeseen events occur. The scenarios themselves also help to stimulate creative thinking and identify potential opportunities that might not be apparent under a single-forecast approach. Regular reviews and adjustments to the scenarios are vital, as new information emerges and the external environment evolves. This iterative process ensures that the organization's plans remain relevant and adaptable.

Agile decision-making processes emphasize speed and flexibility. Traditional hierarchical decision-making can be slow and cumbersome, particularly in rapidly changing circumstances. Agile processes empower teams to make decisions quickly and autonomously, adapting to new information and feedback as it becomes available. These processes often involve iterative cycles of planning, execution, and review, allowing for continuous improvement and adjustment. This iterative approach is particularly effective in managing complex projects or initiatives, where unforeseen challenges or opportunities may arise during implementation.

Effective agile decision-making necessitates strong cross-functional collaboration and clear communication channels. Teams need to be empowered to make decisions within their areas of expertise, while also maintaining alignment with overall organizational objectives. Regular feedback loops are crucial, providing the opportunity to identify and address potential problems early on. The process should be transparent, ensuring that stakeholders are kept informed of decisions and their rationale. Furthermore, the process should encourage experimentation and learning from both successes and failures, fostering a culture of continuous improvement.

Addressing cognitive biases is a crucial element of effective decision-making in uncertain environments. Cognitive biases are systematic errors in thinking that can distort our judgments and lead to poor decisions. Confirmation bias, for instance, involves favoring information that confirms pre-existing beliefs while ignoring contradictory evidence. Anchoring bias refers to over-reliance on the first piece of information received, even if it is irrelevant or outdated. Availability bias leads to overestimating the likelihood of events that are easily recalled, often due to their vividness or recent occurrence.

Groupthink, the tendency for groups to suppress dissenting opinions in favor of consensus, is another common bias.

Mitigating these biases requires a conscious effort to challenge assumptions, seek diverse perspectives, and encourage critical evaluation of information. Techniques such as devil's advocacy (assigning someone to argue against a proposed decision) and pre-mortem analysis (imagining a failed outcome and identifying potential causes) can help to uncover potential flaws in thinking. Encouraging structured decision-making processes, using checklists and decision matrices, can help to reduce the influence of biases by introducing a degree of formality and objectivity. Regular training on cognitive biases and decision-making principles can further enhance awareness and improve judgment.

Making effective decisions in uncertain environments demands a move beyond traditional approaches. Evidence-based decision-making provides a framework for using data rigorously, scenario planning enhances preparedness for unforeseen circumstances, and agile processes enable rapid adaptation. By consciously addressing cognitive biases and fostering a culture of continuous learning and improvement, organizations can significantly enhance their ability to make sound judgments, navigate complexity, and thrive in today's dynamic world. The integration of these frameworks, tailored to the specific context of the organization and the nature of the decisions at hand, will lay the foundation for building a truly agile and resilient enterprise. Adaptability, therefore, is not simply a reaction to change, but a core strategic capability built through deliberate practice and the consistent application of proven decision-making frameworks.

Experimentation and Iterative Improvement

Experimentation, the cornerstone of scientific advancement, finds its equally crucial place within the realm of adaptive leadership. It's no longer sufficient to simply react to change; proactive, data-driven experimentation is essential for navigating the complexities of today's business environment. This involves consciously designing experiments, gathering feedback, and iteratively improving strategies and processes based on the results obtained. This isn't about reckless risk-taking; instead, it's a disciplined approach to learning and adaptation, minimizing potential downsides while maximizing opportunities for growth.

The principles of experimentation and iterative improvement are most prominently showcased in industries that embrace agile methodologies, particularly within software development and product design. These sectors have honed the art of "failing fast," recognizing that rapid iteration, incorporating frequent feedback loops, is significantly more efficient than lengthy resource-intensive projects that might ultimately prove ineffective. Consider the iterative development process employed by many successful software companies. They don't build entire software systems in one go; instead, they develop

Minimum Viable Products (MVPs)– stripped-down versions containing the core functionality.

These MVPs are then released to a select group of users, often through beta testing programs. This allows for immediate feedback on the user experience, enabling developers to identify bugs, usability issues, and areas for improvement early in the development cycle. The feedback gathered from beta testing is invaluable. It highlights both the strengths and weaknesses of the MVP, informing crucial adjustments before a wider release. This iterative process of development, testing, feedback, and refinement continues throughout the project lifecycle.

Instead of a monolithic, "set-it-and-forget-it" approach, agile development embraces continuous adaptation. Changes are made incrementally, with regular releases delivering new features and enhancements based on user input and evolving market demands. This approach significantly reduces the risk of launching a product that fails to meet market expectations, saving valuable time and resources.

This same philosophy extends beyond software development. Product design firms frequently utilize similar techniques, creating prototypes and conducting user testing to refine designs before mass production. For example, a company designing a new ergonomic office chair might create multiple prototypes, each incorporating slightly different features. These prototypes are then tested by target users, whose feedback informs the final design. This iterative approach minimizes the risk of launching a product that is uncomfortable, inefficient, or simply doesn't appeal to consumers. The iterative refinement, driven by data and user feedback, significantly increases the likelihood of creating a commercially successful product.

The concept of "failing fast" is integral to this experimental approach. It doesn't imply a lack of planning or preparation; rather, it emphasizes the importance of learning from mistakes quickly and efficiently. In a rapidly changing business environment, clinging to a failing strategy for too long can be far more detrimental than quickly admitting a misstep and shifting course. The key is to create an environment where experimentation is encouraged, where failure is viewed as a learning opportunity, and where individuals and teams are not penalized for taking calculated risks. This requires a shift in organizational culture, moving away from a blame-oriented approach towards one that fosters open communication and mutual learning.

To successfully implement experimentation and iterative improvement, organizations need to establish clear processes for designing experiments, collecting data, analyzing results, and making adjustments. This involves defining specific, measurable, achievable, relevant, and time-bound (SMART) objectives for each experiment. The metrics used to evaluate the success or failure of an experiment must be clearly defined upfront. For instance, an experiment designed to improve customer satisfaction might measure metrics such as customer satisfaction scores, net promoter scores, or customer churn rates. A company launching a new marketing campaign might track metrics like click-through rates, conversion rates, or return on investment.

The data collected should be analyzed rigorously, using appropriate statistical techniques to identify patterns and trends. This analysis should inform decisions about whether to continue, modify, or abandon an experiment. Furthermore, a system for documenting the results of experiments is crucial. This documentation serves as a valuable repository of knowledge, allowing the organization to learn from past experiences and avoid repeating past mistakes. This knowledge base can inform future experiments, accelerating the learning process and improving the organization's overall agility.

Leadership also plays a critical role in fostering a culture of experimentation. Leaders must encourage their teams to take calculated risks, provide the resources necessary for experimentation, and create a safe space for failure. This means protecting individuals and teams from undue criticism when experiments don't yield the desired results. Instead, the focus should be on analyzing what went wrong, learning from the experience, and using this knowledge to inform future endeavors. This requires a significant shift in mindset, moving away from a culture that prizes perfection and avoids risk towards one that embraces continuous improvement and views experimentation as a key driver of innovation and success.

The application of experimentation extends beyond product development and marketing. It can be applied to various aspects of organizational operations, from streamlining internal processes to improving employee engagement. For example, a company seeking to improve its internal communication might experiment with different communication channels, such as instant messaging, email, or video conferencing. By tracking employee feedback and productivity, the company can identify the most effective communication methods. Similarly, a company looking to boost employee morale might experiment with different employee engagement initiatives, such as team-building activities, employee recognition programs, or flexible work arrangements. By carefully measuring the impact of these initiatives, the company can identify the ones that are most successful in boosting employee morale and productivity.

Experimentation and iterative improvement are not merely optional elements of adaptive leadership; they are essential for thriving in today's dynamic and unpredictable business environment. By embracing a culture of experimentation, organizations can significantly enhance their ability to adapt to change, respond to challenges, and seize opportunities. The principles of "failing fast," learning from mistakes, and continuously refining processes are vital for maintaining a competitive edge and achieving long-term success. The integration of rigorous experimentation and data-driven decision-making allows organizations to not only survive, but flourish amidst uncertainty, establishing a resilient and adaptable foundation for future growth. This constant cycle of experimentation, learning, and adaptation becomes the very lifeblood of a strategically agile organization, ensuring its continued relevance and success in an ever-changing world.

Building a Culture of Experimentation and Learning

Building a culture that thrives on experimentation and learning requires a fundamental shift in mindset, moving away from a fear of failure towards an embrace of continuous improvement. This transition necessitates a multi-pronged approach, addressing both the systemic aspects of organizational structure and the individual attitudes of employees. It's not simply about implementing new processes; it's about cultivating a deep-seated belief in the power of learning through trial and error.

One crucial step is to redefine the perception of failure. Instead of viewing mistakes as setbacks, they must be reframed as invaluable learning opportunities. This requires establishing a psychologically safe environment where individuals feel comfortable taking calculated risks without fear of retribution. This psychological safety is not a passive element; it needs active cultivation by leadership. Leaders must explicitly communicate that experimentation is valued, that mistakes are expected as part of the learning process, and that individuals will not be penalized for taking calculated risks that don't pan out. This means actively celebrating both successes and "smart failures" – failures that provide significant learning opportunities.

This cultural shift is best achieved through clear, consistent messaging and visible actions. Leaders should share personal stories of their own failures and the lessons learned, thereby modeling the desired behavior. This transparency fosters trust and encourages others to be equally open about their own experiences. Moreover, it's essential to establish a formal process for capturing and analyzing the lessons learned from both successful and unsuccessful experiments. This could involve post-experiment reviews, facilitated by experienced members of the organization, where the team discusses what worked, what didn't, and what insights can be gleaned for future endeavors. These reviews should not be punitive; their purpose is to identify actionable insights and improve future efforts.

Implementing a robust system for knowledge sharing is critical. The lessons learned from one experiment shouldn't remain isolated within a single team; they should be disseminated throughout the organization. This might involve creating a central repository where experimental results are documented, analyzed, and made accessible to all employees. Internal communication channels, such as newsletters, intranet articles, or dedicated workshops, can be used to share successful strategies and lessons learned from failures. This collaborative approach ensures that the entire organization benefits from the collective learning, fostering a culture of shared knowledge and continuous improvement.

Beyond individual learning, the structure of the organization itself needs to support a culture of experimentation. This includes providing the necessary resources – time, budget, and personnel – for teams to conduct experiments. Rigid budgeting processes and inflexible project timelines can stifle innovation and experimentation. Organizations should allocate a portion of their resources specifically for experimental projects, recognizing that not all experiments will be successful, but that the collective learning generated will outweigh the cost of occasional failures. Processes must also be streamlined to facilitate rapid iteration. Bureaucratic hurdles and lengthy approval processes can significantly delay the feedback loop, diminishing the effectiveness of experimentation. Organizations should strive to create a more agile and responsive decision-making process, enabling teams to quickly adapt and modify their strategies based on the feedback they receive. This could involve decentralizing decision-making, empowering teams to make quicker decisions without excessive oversight.

Addressing potential resistance to experimentation is another critical aspect. Some individuals or teams may be resistant to change, preferring the comfort of established routines and processes. This resistance stems from various factors, including fear of failure, lack of trust in the leadership, or simply a lack of understanding of the benefits of experimentation. Addressing this resistance requires a multifaceted approach that involves open communication, education, and demonstrating the tangible benefits of experimentation. Leaders need to actively listen to concerns, address anxieties, and clearly articulate the value proposition of a culture of experimentation, highlighting its role in driving innovation and improving organizational performance. Success stories, case studies, and concrete examples of how experimentation has led to positive outcomes can help persuade those hesitant to embrace this new approach.

Finally, leadership plays a pivotal role in fostering a culture of experimentation. Leaders must not only advocate for experimentation but also actively participate in the process. They should be involved in designing experiments, providing guidance and support to teams, and celebrating both successes and learning opportunities from failures. Their active involvement signals the importance of experimentation, reinforcing its value within the organizational culture. Moreover, leaders should foster a culture of psychological safety by encouraging open communication, actively listening to concerns, and creating a space where employees feel comfortable taking calculated risks without fear of negative consequences. This proactive and supportive leadership is paramount in building a sustainable culture of experimentation and continuous improvement.

Building a culture of experimentation and learning is not a one-time project; it's an ongoing journey that requires continuous effort and adaptation. It demands a shift in mindset, a revision of organizational processes, and dedicated commitment from leadership. However, the rewards are substantial. Organizations that successfully cultivate a culture of experimentation are better equipped to adapt to change, navigate uncertainty, and seize opportunities for innovation and growth in a rapidly evolving business landscape. This continuous cycle of learning and improvement becomes a powerful engine driving organizational resilience and long-term success. The ability to adapt, innovate, and learn from failures becomes a core competency, differentiating these organizations from those that remain entrenched in outdated methods and resistant to change. The journey requires consistent effort, ongoing communication, and a willingness to embrace both successes and failures as valuable learning experiences. The ultimate goal is to create an organizational ecosystem that actively seeks out opportunities for improvement, embraces risk, and thrives on the continuous process of experimentation and adaptation. This is the hallmark of a truly agile and resilient organization, prepared to meet the challenges of tomorrow with confidence and adaptability.

Chapter 3: Leading with Empathy and Emotional Intelligence

Understanding the Role of Empathy in Adaptive Leadership

Empathy, often overlooked in discussions of leadership, emerges as a critical component of adaptive leadership, especially during periods of significant organizational change. It's not simply about feeling sorry for others; it's about deeply understanding their perspectives, concerns, and emotions—and responding in ways that demonstrate genuine care and support. In the context of navigating change, empathy facilitates smoother transitions, boosts morale, and unlocks collaborative potential that might otherwise remain untapped. Leaders who demonstrate empathy build trust, fostering an environment where employees feel safe to express their anxieties, share their ideas, and actively participate in shaping the future of the organization.

The importance of empathy in adaptive leadership stems from the inherent anxieties and uncertainties that accompany change. Employees may fear job insecurity, struggle to adapt to new technologies or processes, or grapple with the emotional toll of shifting roles and responsibilities. These feelings are not merely individual quirks; they are legitimate responses to a significant disruption of the status quo. Leaders who disregard these emotional aspects risk creating a climate of mistrust, resentment, and resistance to change. Conversely, leaders who actively listen, acknowledge these concerns, and demonstrate genuine understanding foster a sense of psychological safety, thereby significantly increasing the likelihood of a smooth and successful transition.

Active listening, a cornerstone of empathetic leadership, is more than simply hearing what others are saying. It involves paying close attention to both verbal and nonverbal cues, actively seeking to understand the underlying emotions and perspectives being expressed. This requires leaders to set aside their own biases and assumptions, creating a space for open and honest dialogue. It involves asking clarifying questions, paraphrasing to ensure understanding, and demonstrating genuine interest in the speaker's experience.

For instance, during a town hall meeting announcing a restructuring, an empathetic leader wouldn't simply recite the changes. They would actively solicit questions, acknowledge concerns about job security, and address anxieties directly, demonstrating a willingness to listen and engage with the emotional impact of the changes. This active listening demonstrates respect for employees' feelings and positions them as valued partners in the change process.

Understanding diverse perspectives is another critical element of empathetic leadership. Organizations are made up of individuals with varying backgrounds, experiences, and viewpoints. During times of change, these differences can lead to conflicts and misunderstandings. Empathetic leaders recognize the importance of acknowledging these diverse perspectives and creating a space where everyone feels heard and valued. This involves actively seeking out input from a wide range of employees, valuing their contributions, and incorporating their concerns into decision-making processes. For example, when implementing a new software system, an empathetic leader would consult with employees from different departments, taking into account their unique needs and challenges. Failing to do so could result in a system that is poorly adapted to the needs of the users, leading to frustration, inefficiency, and ultimately, resistance to the change.

Demonstrating genuine care for employees goes beyond simply acknowledging their concerns. It involves actively seeking ways to support their well-being and address their needs during times of change. This might involve providing additional training and development opportunities, offering counseling services, or establishing clear communication channels to keep employees informed and engaged. It also requires leaders to be visible and approachable, making themselves available to answer questions and provide support. For example, a leader might schedule one-on-one meetings with employees to discuss their concerns and provide individualized support, demonstrating their commitment to their well-being. This personalized attention can significantly boost morale and increase employee engagement, which is critical for successfully navigating change.

Developing empathy is not an innate trait; it's a skill that can be cultivated through conscious effort and practice. Leaders can enhance their empathy by actively seeking opportunities to understand others' perspectives, engaging in conversations with individuals from diverse backgrounds, and actively listening to their stories. Empathy is developed through a continuous process of self-reflection, actively seeking feedback from others, and making conscious efforts to improve understanding. Leaders can attend workshops or training programs that focus on emotional intelligence and empathy building, further enhancing their leadership capabilities. Regular mindfulness practices can help improve emotional awareness and deepen understanding of the emotional states of others. By actively listening and validating employee concerns, leaders create a safer environment fostering a culture of trust and cooperation, greatly enhancing the likelihood of a successful change process.

The impact of empathetic leadership during change is profound. Research consistently demonstrates a strong correlation between empathetic leadership and improved employee morale, productivity, and overall organizational performance. Employees who feel understood and supported are more likely to be engaged, motivated, and committed to the success of the organization. This translates to improved team dynamics, increased innovation, and reduced resistance to change. Conversely, a lack of empathy can lead to decreased morale, increased stress, and higher employee turnover rates, all of which can negatively impact organizational effectiveness. Thus, the ability to lead with empathy becomes a strategic advantage, enabling organizations to navigate change more effectively and emerge stronger and more resilient.

Many successful leaders have demonstrated the power of empathy in navigating organizational change. Consider leaders who have successfully led their organizations through mergers, acquisitions, or restructuring. These leaders often demonstrate an exceptional ability to understand and address the emotional needs of their employees. They may actively listen to concerns about job security, provide clear and transparent communication, and offer support and guidance during the transition period. This demonstrates a commitment to the well-being of their employees, building trust and increasing the likelihood of a successful transition.

Their empathy isn't a soft skill, but a crucial leadership competency. It allows them to create an environment where employees feel valued and respected, even during significant organizational change. These leaders demonstrate that empathetic leadership isn't simply a "nice-to-have"; it's a critical driver of organizational success.

Their stories serve as powerful case studies, showcasing the tangible benefits of leading with empathy and emotional intelligence. In the context of adaptive leadership, this becomes essential for maintaining a positive, productive workforce, capable of embracing change and effectively contributing to the organization's ongoing success. The ability to lead with empathy and emotional intelligence is not merely a desirable trait; it's a critical competency for leaders navigating the complexities of a dynamic and ever-changing world. It empowers leaders to build strong, resilient teams, fostering a culture of trust, collaboration, and continuous improvement– all essential for successfully navigating the challenges of the future. The intentional development and application of empathy is, therefore, not a matter of choice but a strategic imperative for achieving sustainable organizational success in the modern age.

Developing Emotional Intelligence for Effective Communication

Developing emotional intelligence is no longer a "nice-to-have" but a critical competency for leaders navigating the complexities of organizational change. It's the cornerstone of effective communication, allowing leaders to connect meaningfully with their teams and guide them through uncertainty. This goes beyond simply understanding emotions; it's about harnessing emotional intelligence to build trust, manage conflict, and foster a culture of open communication. This subsection looks into the four key components of emotional intelligence and provides practical strategies for enhancing them within the context of leadership and organizational change.

First, *self-awareness* forms the foundation of emotional intelligence. This involves understanding one's own emotions, strengths, weaknesses, values, and motivations. A self-aware leader recognizes how their emotions influence their behavior and decision-making, and how these, in turn, impact their team. During times of change, self-awareness helps leaders manage their own anxieties and stress, preventing these feelings from negatively affecting their communication and leadership. For instance, a self-aware leader undergoing a company restructure might recognize their own feelings of insecurity and proactively address them before communicating changes to their team, thus preventing the projection of their anxieties onto their employees. Self-awareness involves regular introspection, seeking feedback from trusted sources, and actively reflecting on one's reactions in various situations. This can be cultivated through practices like journaling, mindfulness meditation, or seeking regular feedback from trusted mentors or colleagues. Honest self-assessment tools can also be extremely beneficial. Understanding one's emotional triggers and how they impact interactions lays the groundwork for effective communication during periods of change.

Building on self-awareness is *self-regulation*, the ability to manage one's own emotions and impulses. This is crucial during times of organizational change when stress and uncertainty can lead to emotional outbursts or impulsive decisions. Self-regulation enables leaders to remain calm, composed, and objective, even in the face of challenging situations. A leader demonstrating self-regulation might calmly address concerns during a difficult meeting, responding thoughtfully to criticism instead of reacting defensively. This creates a safe and respectful environment where team members feel comfortable expressing their thoughts and feelings without fear of reprisal. Practical strategies for self-regulation include deep breathing exercises, mindfulness practices, and developing coping mechanisms for stress. Setting clear boundaries, prioritizing self-care, and understanding personal stress triggers are also essential elements of effective self-regulation. Leaders who master self-regulation are better equipped to navigate the emotional turbulence of change and maintain a positive and productive work environment.

The third component, *social awareness,* involves understanding and empathizing with the emotions, needs, and perspectives of others. This is deeply interconnected with empathy, a quality crucial for adaptive leadership. It requires actively listening to team members, observing their nonverbal cues, and attempting to understand their emotional responses to change. A leader displaying social awareness will notice an employee's hesitation during a meeting and proactively engage them to uncover the reasons for their reticence. This ability to read and respond to the emotional cues of others is critical for building trust and rapport, especially during periods of organizational transformation. Effective social awareness involves paying attention to both verbal and nonverbal communication, asking clarifying questions, actively seeking out diverse perspectives, and demonstrating genuine curiosity in the experiences of others. Improving social awareness can involve actively practicing listening skills, observing body language, and consciously seeking out opportunities to interact with individuals from different backgrounds and perspectives.

Finally, *relationship management* is the ability to build and maintain positive relationships with others. This involves using emotional intelligence to influence and inspire, effectively managing conflict, and collaborating effectively within a team. During organizational change, relationship management helps leaders build consensus, foster cooperation, and navigate conflicts that might arise. A leader adept at relationship management will facilitate collaborative problem-solving sessions during periods of uncertainty, effectively mediating disagreements and creating a shared vision for the future. This proactive approach prevents minor conflicts from escalating and ensures the organization's ability to adapt collaboratively. Effective relationship management requires strong communication skills, active listening, empathy, and the ability to build trust. It also involves recognizing and addressing differing perspectives and building strong relationships with individuals from various backgrounds. Practical strategies include actively seeking feedback, providing constructive criticism, and building rapport through shared experiences and open dialogue. Furthermore, conflict resolution training can equip leaders with effective strategies for resolving disagreements constructively and fairly.

Enhancing emotional intelligence is not a passive process; it requires conscious effort and consistent practice. Leaders can significantly improve their emotional intelligence through a combination of self-reflection, training, and mindful practice. Regular self-assessment exercises, combined with feedback from trusted colleagues, can highlight areas for improvement. Workshops and training programs specifically focused on emotional intelligence can equip leaders with practical tools and strategies for enhancing their skills. Mindfulness practices, such as meditation and deep breathing exercises, can enhance self-awareness and emotional regulation. Actively seeking out opportunities to engage with individuals from diverse backgrounds and perspectives can significantly improve social awareness. By integrating these practices into their daily routines, leaders can cultivate a higher level of emotional intelligence, resulting in more effective communication, stronger relationships, and greater success in navigating organizational change.

The benefits of high emotional intelligence in leadership during change are undeniable. It fosters a culture of trust, transparency, and collaboration, leading to higher levels of employee engagement, improved morale, and increased productivity. It empowers leaders to manage conflict effectively, preventing minor disagreements from escalating into larger issues. It facilitates open communication channels, allowing employees to voice their concerns and contribute to the change process. Leaders who demonstrate high emotional intelligence are more likely to build strong relationships with their teams, fostering a sense of psychological safety where employees feel comfortable sharing their thoughts and feelings without fear of retribution. This shared understanding promotes a sense of team cohesion and collective purpose, fostering resilience and adaptability during periods of organizational uncertainty.

Emotional intelligence is not merely a desirable attribute for leaders; it is a critical competency for effective leadership during times of change. By developing self-awareness, self-regulation, social awareness, and relationship management skills, leaders can foster open communication, build strong relationships, and effectively navigate the complexities of organizational transformation. This enhanced leadership style results in a more engaged, productive, and resilient workforce, ultimately leading to the successful and smooth implementation of any change initiative. Investing time and effort in developing emotional intelligence is not just an investment in individual leadership skills but a strategic investment in the organization's overall success and long-term sustainability. It is an investment that yields significant returns in terms of improved morale, reduced resistance to change, and enhanced organizational effectiveness in the face of ongoing challenges.

Building Trust and Psychological Safety within Teams

Building trust and psychological safety is paramount, particularly within teams undergoing significant change. Without these foundational elements, even the most well-intentioned initiatives can falter. Resistance to change, decreased productivity, and high turnover are all potential consequences of a team environment lacking trust and psychological safety. These are not merely "soft skills"; they are critical leadership competencies that directly impact the bottom line.

Trust, at its core, is the belief in the reliability, truth, and ability of others. In a team context, it's the confidence that team members have in each other's competence, integrity, and commitment to the shared goals. This isn't a passive state; it's actively cultivated through consistent behavior and demonstrated actions over time. Psychological safety, on the other hand, refers to a shared belief held by team members that the team is a safe place for interpersonal risk-taking. It's the assurance that individuals can express their opinions, ask questions, admit mistakes, and offer suggestions without fear of negative consequences, such as ridicule, punishment, or marginalization. Both trust and psychological safety are intertwined; one cannot truly exist without the other. A team can have high trust but lack psychological safety if individuals feel punished for expressing dissenting viewpoints or voicing concerns.

One of the primary drivers of trust and psychological safety is open communication. This goes beyond simply holding regular meetings; it requires creating a culture where information flows freely, both up and down the organizational hierarchy. Transparency is key – team members need to understand the "why" behind decisions, even if they don't agree with them. This transparency fosters a sense of inclusion and shared purpose, making individuals feel valued and informed. It's also important to actively solicit feedback from team members at all levels. Regular feedback mechanisms, such as anonymous surveys, suggestion boxes, or one-on-one meetings, can provide invaluable insights into team dynamics and identify potential roadblocks to trust. This feedback shouldn't be seen as a threat, but as an opportunity for continuous improvement and growth. Leaders must be receptive to and act upon that feedback; dismissing concerns or ignoring suggestions undermines trust instantly.

Mutual respect is another essential ingredient. This means valuing the contributions of each team member, regardless of their role or seniority. Acknowledging and celebrating both individual and team accomplishments fosters a positive and collaborative environment. Conversely, belittling contributions, openly criticizing individuals, or displaying favoritism erodes trust and creates an atmosphere of fear and insecurity. Leaders should lead by example, treating everyone with fairness and courtesy, actively listening to diverse perspectives, and valuing different approaches to problem-solving. Creating opportunities for team members to interact outside of formal work settings, such as team-building activities or informal social gatherings, can also foster camaraderie and mutual understanding. These activities aren't merely frivolous additions; they serve to build relationships and create bonds that strengthen the team's resilience during stressful times.

However, creating trust and psychological safety isn't a passive process; it demands proactive and consistent effort from leadership. One effective strategy is to actively address concerns and grievances promptly and fairly. This demonstrates a commitment to transparency and accountability, showing team members that their voices matter. Leaders should establish clear and consistent processes for handling complaints and disputes, ensuring that all team members are treated equitably. Fostering a culture of psychological safety requires actively encouraging risk-taking and embracing failure as a learning opportunity. This means providing a space where individuals feel comfortable challenging the status quo, experimenting with new ideas, and admitting mistakes without fear of retribution. Leading by example, admitting personal mistakes, and openly discussing setbacks are critical steps to creating this culture.

Providing regular feedback is essential, not only to gauge team members' perceptions but also to correct misunderstandings and reinforce positive behaviors. This feedback must be delivered constructively, focusing on specific behaviors rather than making personal attacks. It should also be balanced, acknowledging both strengths and areas for improvement. Providing feedback in a timely manner ensures that issues are addressed promptly, preventing them from escalating. Regular performance reviews, combined with informal feedback sessions, provide opportunities for open dialogue and demonstrate leadership's commitment to team members' growth and development.

Case studies illustrate the profound impact of trust and psychological safety on organizational success. Consider companies that have successfully navigated significant mergers or acquisitions. Those with strong pre-existing cultures of trust and psychological safety within individual teams generally experienced smoother transitions and better integration of the two organizations. The existing open communication and mutual respect facilitated the sharing of information and the collaborative problem-solving necessary to address the inevitable challenges of a merger. Conversely, organizations that lacked these elements often experienced higher levels of conflict, resistance, and ultimately, a longer and more painful integration process. Successful change management initiatives often rely on the ability of teams to adapt swiftly and effectively. Teams lacking trust and psychological safety are less likely to adapt quickly due to heightened anxiety and resistance to change.

Building trust and psychological safety is an ongoing process, not a destination. It requires continuous effort and commitment from leaders at all levels. Regularly assessing team dynamics, soliciting feedback, and actively addressing issues are critical for maintaining a healthy and productive work environment. Leaders who prioritize building trust and psychological safety create a strong foundation for adaptability, innovation, and organizational resilience in the face of any challenge. The resulting benefits extend far beyond improved morale and reduced turnover; they translate directly into increased productivity, improved innovation, and greater organizational success. By investing in these essential elements, organizations are not merely improving their working environment; they are enhancing their capacity to thrive in today's dynamic business landscape. The return on this investment is not simply measured in financial terms, but in the overall well-being and success of the organization and its people. The creation of a psychologically safe workplace isn't a soft skill; it's a strategic imperative for survival and growth.

Managing Conflict and Navigating Difficult Conversations

Conflict is inevitable in any team, especially during periods of significant change. The pressures of adaptation, coupled with differing perspectives and working styles, can easily escalate disagreements. However, the manner in which conflict is handled significantly impacts the overall success of the change initiative. Instead of viewing conflict as inherently negative, leaders should recognize it as an opportunity for growth, innovation, and enhanced team cohesion. The key lies in managing conflict constructively, transforming potential friction into a catalyst for collaboration and improved understanding.

Effective conflict management begins with proactive measures aimed at preventing conflicts before they escalate. This involves establishing clear communication channels, ensuring transparency in decision-making processes, and fostering a culture of mutual respect. Regular check-ins, team meetings dedicated to open dialogue, and the establishment of clear guidelines for problem-solving all contribute to a more proactive approach. When issues do arise, a well-defined conflict resolution process can significantly minimize disruption and facilitate a positive resolution.

Central to managing conflict effectively is the ability to engage in difficult conversations with empathy and emotional intelligence. This is not about avoiding conflict, but about navigating it with skill and sensitivity. The first step is active listening— truly hearing and understanding the other person's perspective, without interrupting or formulating a rebuttal. This requires consciously putting aside pre-conceived notions and biases, focusing instead on understanding the underlying emotions and concerns driving the other person's viewpoint. Paraphrasing what has been said and asking clarifying questions to demonstrate genuine interest and enhance understanding. Active listening validates the other person's feelings, creating a safer space for open dialogue.

Once both parties feel heard and understood, a respectful dialogue can commence. This means expressing one's own perspective clearly and concisely, but without resorting to accusatory language or personal attacks. Focusing on the issue at hand, rather than on personalities, is crucial. Using "I" statements" I feel frustrated when..." or "I am concerned that..."— helps frame the conversation constructively and avoids blaming or shaming others. The goal is to find common ground, not to win an argument.

Effective conflict resolution techniques often involve brainstorming collaborative solutions. Instead of imposing a solution, leaders should facilitate a process where team members work together to identify mutually acceptable options. This collaborative approach encourages ownership and buy-in from all parties involved, improving the likelihood of a successful outcome. Compromise is often necessary, requiring each party to make concessions in order to achieve a shared resolution. However, compromise should never be at the expense of core values or principles. The aim is to find a solution that satisfies the needs of all parties as much as reasonably possible, without sacrificing ethical considerations.

Mediation can be a valuable tool in resolving complex or deeply rooted conflicts. A neutral third party, ideally someone with experience in conflict resolution, can facilitate communication, help identify underlying issues, and guide the parties toward a mutually acceptable solution. Mediation helps prevent the conflict from escalating into personal attacks or damaging the overall team dynamic. A skilled mediator can help maintain a respectful and productive dialogue, ensuring that the process remains focused on finding a resolution rather than assigning blame.

Following the resolution of a conflict, it's critical to review the process and learn from the experience. This involves reflecting on the strengths and weaknesses of the conflict management approach, identifying areas for improvement in communication, and establishing mechanisms for preventing similar conflicts in the future. Post-conflict discussions should not be punitive, but rather focused on identifying potential systemic issues that contributed to the conflict and developing strategies to mitigate these issues. Documentation of this process can help establish best practices and a common understanding of the organizational approach to conflict resolution, strengthening future responses.

Integrating conflict resolution strategies into leadership training programs is essential. This equips leaders with the necessary skills and tools to effectively navigate difficult conversations and foster a more positive and collaborative work environment. Role-playing exercises and case studies can provide valuable practical experience, allowing leaders to practice techniques in a safe and supportive environment. Training should emphasize the importance of empathy, active listening, and collaborative problem-solving, reinforcing the idea that conflict can be a catalyst for positive change.

Effective conflict management is not a quick fix; it requires ongoing effort and commitment from leaders at all levels. Creating a culture of open communication, mutual respect, and psychological safety is paramount. This involves regularly assessing team dynamics, soliciting feedback from team members, and actively addressing concerns. Leaders must lead by example, demonstrating a willingness to engage in difficult conversations, model appropriate behavior, and accept constructive criticism. This consistent commitment demonstrates the value the organization places on its employees and fosters trust, ultimately leading to a more collaborative, innovative, and resilient team.

Consider the example of a software development team undergoing a significant technological shift. Resistance from some team members, rooted in fear of redundancy or unfamiliar technologies, creates tension and hinders the smooth transition. Instead of dismissing their concerns, a skilled leader would initiate open dialogues, actively listen to their anxieties, and address them with empathy and understanding. They would create a space for open discussion, demonstrating the value of their existing skills and providing training and support for acquiring new ones. This approach prevents conflict from escalating, fostering trust and collaboration as the team collectively tackles the technological shift.

Another example involves a marketing team facing conflicting strategies regarding a new product launch. Different team members advocate for different approaches, leading to heated debates and potential deadlock. A skilled leader facilitates a structured brainstorming session, encouraging each team member to present their ideas and rationale. Active listening helps to identify common goals and underlying concerns. This collaborative approach ultimately leads to a blended strategy that incorporates elements from each individual proposal, fostering a sense of shared ownership and promoting a unified team effort. The key is creating an environment where everyone feels valued, empowered to voice their opinions, and contributing to a successful outcome.

Conversely, consider organizations where conflict is avoided or repressed. Unresolved issues fester, creating a breeding ground for resentment and mistrust. This negativity can significantly impede productivity, hinder innovation, and ultimately damage the organization's culture. Such a climate leads to disengaged employees, increased turnover, and reduced organizational effectiveness. Therefore, proactive conflict management is not merely a best practice; it's a strategic imperative for success. Organizations that prioritize effective conflict resolution demonstrate a greater ability to navigate change, adapt to new challenges, and achieve long-term sustainability. This translates not only to improved operational efficiency and profitability, but to a significantly more positive and productive work environment for all.

The impact of effective conflict management extends beyond immediate team dynamics. Successful navigation of difficult conversations strengthens relationships, fosters mutual respect, and builds a foundation for future collaboration. This ultimately results in a more cohesive and resilient team, better equipped to handle future challenges and contribute to the overall success of the organization. Therefore, by investing in conflict resolution skills and fostering a culture of open communication and mutual understanding, organizations are not just resolving immediate problems; they are building a foundation for sustainable growth and long-term success. The payoff extends far beyond the resolution of a specific conflict; it strengthens the team, enhances trust, and cultivates a culture where challenges are faced collaboratively and opportunities for growth are maximized.

Fostering Collaboration and Teamwork in Dynamic Environments

Building high-performing teams in constantly shifting environments requires a multifaceted approach that transcends simple task delegation. It necessitates cultivating a culture of trust, open communication, and shared understanding, all underpinned by a strong sense of collective purpose. This isn't merely about assembling a group of skilled individuals; it's about forging a cohesive unit capable of adapting and thriving amidst uncertainty.

One crucial element is effective delegation. This isn't about simply assigning tasks; it's about empowering team members by entrusting them with responsibility and autonomy. Successful delegation begins with a clear understanding of each team member's strengths, skills, and aspirations. Leaders should assess individual capabilities and align tasks accordingly, providing opportunities for growth and development. This process involves not just identifying the *what* but also the *how* and the *why,* ensuring everyone understands the context and significance of their contribution to the overall objective. Regular check-ins provide opportunities for feedback, adjustments, and ongoing support, preventing misunderstandings and fostering a sense of ownership.

Fostering a culture of open and honest communication is paramount. This involves creating safe spaces where team members feel comfortable expressing their ideas, concerns, and perspectives without fear of judgment or retribution.

Regular team meetings, both formal and informal, provide platforms for dialogue and knowledge sharing. These shouldn't be mere updates on progress; they should be opportunities for collaborative problem-solving, brainstorming, and mutual support. The use of collaborative tools and platforms can further enhance communication, allowing for real-time collaboration and seamless information flow. Transparent decision-making processes, where team members are involved in shaping the direction of projects, foster a sense of ownership and commitment.

Beyond communication, building a shared sense of purpose is vital. When team members understand how their individual contributions align with broader organizational goals, their commitment and motivation increase significantly. Leaders should clearly articulate the vision and mission, ensuring that every team member understands the "bigger picture" and their role in achieving it. This requires connecting individual tasks to the overarching strategy, highlighting the significance and impact of their efforts. Celebrating successes, both big and small, reinforces this shared purpose and builds team morale. This shared understanding transcends individual tasks; it fosters a sense of collective identity and shared responsibility.

Managing diverse perspectives is another critical aspect of building collaborative teams. In today's globally interconnected world, teams are increasingly diverse in terms of backgrounds, experiences, and perspectives. This diversity can be a significant source of innovation and creativity, but it also presents challenges in terms of communication and conflict management. Leaders must actively cultivate an inclusive environment where all voices are heard and respected. This involves implementing strategies for promoting inclusivity, such as establishing clear guidelines for respectful communication, providing training on cultural sensitivity, and actively seeking diverse perspectives in decision-making processes. Creating a sense of psychological safety ensures that team members feel comfortable expressing their opinions, even if they differ from the majority.

To illustrate the power of effective teamwork, consider the example of a medical research team developing a new vaccine. The team consists of virologists, immunologists, chemists, and clinical trial specialists, each with unique expertise and perspectives. The success of the vaccine development hinges not just on individual contributions but on their seamless integration and collaboration. Regular meetings, clear communication channels, and a shared understanding of the overall goals ensure that every member understands their role and how it contributes to the larger objective. The ability to manage diverse perspectives, navigate conflicts constructively, and leverage the strengths of each member is crucial for achieving the team's ambitious goal. The development and launch of successful new products are frequently dependent on this type of cross-functional collaboration.

In contrast, consider a marketing team struggling to launch a new product. Lack of clear communication, conflicting priorities, and a lack of shared understanding lead to delays, missed deadlines, and a fragmented marketing strategy. The absence of a cohesive team dynamic results in a less effective product launch. This situation emphasizes the critical need for proactive leadership in fostering collaboration and ensuring the successful execution of projects, emphasizing the importance of proactive team building and leadership. This contrasts sharply with the success of collaborative ventures where clear communication and shared goals form the backbone of the operation.

The benefits of fostering collaboration and teamwork extend far beyond project success. High-performing teams are more innovative, more resilient, and more adaptable to change. They provide a supportive and enriching environment for individual growth and development, leading to higher job satisfaction and employee retention. This positive work environment also enhances the organization's overall culture, attracting and retaining top talent. Building a collaborative team is therefore not just a matter of operational efficiency; it's an investment in the long-term health and success of the organization.

The process of building collaborative teams is an ongoing journey, not a destination. It requires continuous effort, adaptation, and refinement based on feedback and ongoing evaluation. Leaders must consistently assess team dynamics, identify areas for improvement, and implement strategies to enhance collaboration. This proactive approach strengthens team cohesion, builds resilience, and ultimately contributes to a more successful and fulfilling work environment. By emphasizing the importance of effective communication, shared purpose, and inclusive leadership, organizations can cultivate high-performing teams capable of achieving ambitious goals and thriving in today's dynamic environment. This sustained effort pays off not only in project successes but also in increased employee morale, improved retention, and a more positive and productive organizational culture.

Effective collaboration also requires understanding and embracing different communication styles. Some individuals prefer direct, concise communication, while others favor more nuanced and indirect approaches. A leader skilled in emotional intelligence recognizes these differences and adapts their communication style to ensure that everyone feels heard and understood. This might involve employing visual aids for those who are visually oriented or allowing more time for discussion for those who prefer a more collaborative approach. Similarly, recognizing and respecting different working styles – whether someone thrives in a structured environment or prefers a more flexible approach – allows leaders to create a team dynamic where everyone can contribute effectively.

Fostering psychological safety is crucial for effective collaboration. Team members need to feel comfortable taking risks, sharing their ideas, and admitting mistakes without fear of retribution. A leader who creates a culture of trust and respect encourages open dialogue and constructive feedback, allowing for collaborative problem-solving and continuous improvement. This safe space allows for the free flow of creative ideas and honest feedback, leading to enhanced innovation and improved outcomes. Without this sense of safety, team members may withhold their ideas, hindering creative problem-solving and potentially jeopardizing the overall success of the project.

Building truly collaborative teams demands a long-term commitment to fostering a positive and supportive work environment. This involves regular team-building activities, informal social gatherings, and opportunities for team members to connect on a personal level. These activities strengthen relationships, foster trust, and create a sense of camaraderie. This positive team dynamic leads to improved morale, increased productivity, and ultimately, a more effective and successful team. The investment in fostering these relationships builds a more robust team, better able to navigate challenges and achieve collective success.

Fostering collaboration and teamwork in dynamic environments requires more than just assembling a skilled workforce; it demands a proactive and multifaceted approach to leadership, communication, and team dynamics. By actively promoting effective communication, building a shared sense of purpose, managing diverse perspectives, and fostering a culture of trust and psychological safety, leaders can cultivate high-performing teams capable of navigating complexity, adapting to change, and achieving ambitious goals. This commitment to building collaborative teams translates into significant long-term benefits, enhancing not only organizational success but also the overall well-being and job satisfaction of team members. The result is a more resilient, innovative, and ultimately, more successful organization.

Chapter 4: Cultivating a Culture of Adaptability

Defining and Assessing Organizational Culture

Understanding and assessing organizational culture is paramount to fostering adaptability. A culture that values innovation, experimentation, and learning is far more likely to weather the storms of rapid change than one entrenched in rigid hierarchies and risk aversion. The first step in cultivating a culture of adaptability is to thoroughly understand the existing culture – its strengths, weaknesses, and how it currently impacts the organization's ability to respond to change. This isn't a simple task; it requires a multi-faceted approach, employing various methods to gain a comprehensive understanding.

One effective method is conducting employee surveys. These surveys should go beyond simple satisfaction questionnaires and dive into the specific behaviors and attitudes that influence adaptability. For example, questions could assess the frequency of open communication, the level of trust among team members, the perceived willingness of leadership to embrace new ideas, and the perceived consequences of taking risks. It's crucial to design these surveys carefully, ensuring anonymity and providing clear explanations of the purpose of the assessment. The data gathered should be analyzed not just for overall trends but also for variations across different departments, teams, and levels of seniority. This granularity allows for a more targeted understanding of where cultural changes are most needed.

Alongside employee surveys, conducting interviews with key stakeholders – including employees at all levels, managers, and senior leaders – provides valuable qualitative data. These interviews should probe deeper into the lived experiences of individuals within the organization, exploring their perceptions of the organizational culture and how it affects their ability to adapt to change. Open-ended questions allow for more nuanced responses and the identification of themes and patterns that might not be captured in a quantitative survey. For instance, an interview might reveal that despite positive feedback in surveys, a fear of failure underlies a reluctance to implement innovative ideas, highlighting a critical gap between perception and reality.

Observation is another crucial element of cultural assessment. By observing team meetings, decision-making processes, and daily interactions, consultants can gain firsthand insights into the organization's operational culture. Do meetings tend to be dominated by a few individuals, or is there active participation from all members? Are decisions made in a top-down manner, or is there a more collaborative and inclusive approach? Are mistakes seen as learning opportunities, or are they met with blame and retribution? These observations provide concrete evidence of the culture in action, complementing the insights gained from surveys and interviews. For example, observing a consistently top-down decision-making process may reveal a significant impediment to rapid adaptation.

Beyond these primary methods, reviewing existing organizational documents – such as mission statements, strategic plans, performance reviews, and communication materials – provides additional context. These documents often reveal the organization's stated values and priorities, which can be compared to the reality observed through surveys, interviews, and observations. Discrepancies between stated values and actual behavior highlight areas where cultural alignment is needed. For example, a mission statement that emphasizes innovation but where performance reviews focus solely on efficiency might indicate a dissonance between rhetoric and reality, hindering adaptive capabilities.

In assessing the current cultural state, several key dimensions should be considered. Firstly, the communication style within the organization is crucial. Is communication open, transparent, and two-way, or is it top-down, siloed, and opaque? Organizations with highly adaptable cultures foster open and honest communication at all levels, allowing for the rapid dissemination of information and the free exchange of ideas. Secondly, the decision-making processes play a significant role. Are decisions centralized or decentralized?

Are there established processes for evaluating risks and making timely decisions, or is there a tendency towards slow, bureaucratic processes? Agile decision-making is vital for responding effectively to change. Thirdly, the reward and recognition systems need to be examined. Do they reward innovation and risk-taking, or do they primarily incentivize conformity and adherence to established procedures? Reward systems must align with the desired cultural values.

Fourthly, the level of psychological safety influences willingness to embrace change. Do employees feel comfortable sharing their ideas, taking risks, and admitting mistakes without fear of reprisal? Psychological safety is the cornerstone of a culture that embraces experimentation and learning from failures.

Once the existing culture has been assessed, a comprehensive report should be prepared, summarizing the findings and identifying specific areas for improvement. This report should clearly articulate the existing cultural strengths and weaknesses, linking them directly to the organization's ability to adapt to change. The report should also offer concrete recommendations for cultural change, incorporating insights from relevant case studies of other organizations that have successfully cultivated cultures of adaptability. This includes clearly defining measurable objectives for cultural change, outlining specific strategies to achieve those objectives, and outlining a process for tracking progress and measuring success.

For example, consider an organization that finds its culture is overly risk-averse and resistant to change during its cultural assessment. The report should outline the detrimental effects of this risk aversion on innovation and adaptability, offering concrete recommendations to modify reward systems, leadership training programs, and communication strategies to foster a more experimental culture. The report would include specific, measurable goals, such as increasing the number of innovative ideas implemented per year or reducing the time taken to make critical decisions, outlining a clear path towards transforming the organization's cultural landscape. The success of this initiative would then be tracked and evaluated through ongoing surveys, observations, and employee feedback.

The process of defining and assessing organizational culture is an iterative one, requiring continuous monitoring and adjustment. The initial assessment provides a baseline, but ongoing feedback mechanisms, such as regular pulse surveys and feedback sessions, are needed to track progress and ensure the cultural changes are having the desired impact. This ongoing assessment allows for agile adjustments to the change strategy, preventing the implementation of ineffective initiatives and ensuring the organization remains on track towards becoming more adaptive and resilient. The long-term success of fostering a culture of adaptability hinges upon this continuous evaluation and adaptation. It's not a one-time project but an ongoing commitment to continuous improvement, reflection, and adaptation. This sustained effort will ultimately contribute to the organization's long-term success and viability in an increasingly dynamic environment.

Building a Culture of Continuous Learning and Improvement

Building a culture of continuous learning and improvement is not merely a desirable trait; it's the lifeblood of an adaptable organization. In today's volatile landscape, the ability to learn, adapt, and improve continuously is no longer a competitive advantage—it's a prerequisite for survival. This requires a fundamental shift in mindset, moving away from a fixed, static approach to a dynamic, growth-oriented one. This transition necessitates a multifaceted strategy, encompassing structural changes, leadership commitment, and a deep-seated cultural transformation.

One critical element is fostering a culture of psychological safety. This means creating an environment where employees feel comfortable taking risks, experimenting with new ideas, and admitting mistakes without fear of retribution. When individuals feel safe to fail, they are more likely to embrace challenges, learn from their experiences, and contribute innovative solutions. Conversely, a culture of blame and punishment stifles creativity and innovation, hindering the organization's capacity to adapt and improve. Creating this environment requires a conscious effort from leadership to model vulnerability, encourage open communication, and celebrate both successes and failures as learning opportunities.

Implementing effective feedback mechanisms is crucial for continuous learning. Traditional annual performance reviews often fall short, providing feedback that is infrequent, generalized, and often perceived as punitive. To foster a culture of continuous improvement, organizations should adopt more frequent, informal feedback processes. This could include regular check-ins between managers and employees, peer-to-peer feedback sessions, and 360-degree feedback systems, which solicit input from multiple sources.

The key is to make feedback a regular part of the work process, providing employees with ongoing opportunities to learn and improve. The feedback itself should be constructive, focusing on specific behaviors and offering actionable suggestions for improvement. Crucially, it should be delivered with empathy and a focus on growth, rather than criticism.

Investing in training and development opportunities is paramount to building a learning organization. This involves providing employees with access to a wide range of learning resources, including online courses, workshops, mentoring programs, and external conferences. The training should be tailored to the organization's specific needs and the employees' individual career goals. It's important to move beyond simply providing training and to create a culture where learning is valued and encouraged. This could involve allocating dedicated time for learning during the workday, encouraging employees to attend industry events, and rewarding individuals who actively pursue professional development. The investment in training shouldn't be viewed as a cost but rather as an investment in the organization's future.

Creating opportunities for knowledge sharing and collaboration is another critical step. Knowledge resides not just within individual employees but also within teams and across the organization. Fostering a culture of knowledge sharing enables the rapid dissemination of information and best practices, accelerating the learning process and improving organizational performance. This can be achieved through various methods, such as establishing internal knowledge bases, creating communities of practice, and encouraging employees to share their expertise through presentations, workshops, or informal mentoring. The goal is to create a system where knowledge flows freely throughout the organization, enabling rapid adaptation and continuous improvement.

Furthermore, organizations should actively encourage experimentation and innovation. A culture of continuous improvement embraces failure as a learning opportunity. Experimentation inevitably leads to some failures, but these failures provide valuable insights that can be used to improve future efforts. Organizations should create a space where employees feel comfortable taking calculated risks, trying new approaches, and learning from their mistakes.

This requires a shift in mindset from blame to learning, where failures are viewed as opportunities for growth and development. Creating a culture of experimentation also necessitates establishing clear processes for evaluating the results of experiments, learning from both successes and failures, and adapting future strategies accordingly. This iterative process of experimentation and learning is fundamental to continuous improvement.

Beyond internal initiatives, actively seeking external knowledge and best practices is equally crucial. Benchmarking against other organizations, attending industry conferences, and participating in professional networks can provide valuable insights and inspiration. By learning from others' successes and failures, organizations can avoid repeating past mistakes and accelerate their own learning process. Fostering relationships with external partners, such as universities, research institutions, and other organizations, can provide access to cutting-edge knowledge and expertise, enhancing the organization's capacity for innovation and adaptation.

A vital component of building a culture of continuous learning is the active involvement of leadership. Leaders must not only espouse the values of learning and improvement but also model these behaviors. This involves actively participating in learning initiatives, seeking feedback from employees, and demonstrating a willingness to learn and adapt. Leaders should create a climate where learning is valued, encouraged, and rewarded. They should also allocate resources to support learning initiatives and communicate the importance of continuous learning to all employees. This visible commitment from leadership sets the tone for the entire organization, ensuring that learning becomes an integral part of the organizational culture.

Measuring and tracking progress is essential to ensure the effectiveness of continuous learning initiatives. Key performance indicators (KPIs) should be established to track the impact of these initiatives on organizational performance. This could include metrics such as employee satisfaction, employee engagement, innovation rates, and the rate of successful implementation of new ideas. Regularly reviewing these KPIs allows organizations to assess the effectiveness of their learning initiatives and make adjustments as needed. The data gathered should be used to inform future learning and development strategies, ensuring that the organization continuously improves its capacity for adaptation.

Finally, embedding continuous learning into the organization's strategic planning process is vital. It shouldn't be a separate initiative but an integral part of the organization's overall goals and objectives. This means integrating learning objectives into performance reviews, incorporating learning activities into the annual budget, and making continuous learning a key performance indicator for managers and employees alike. By embedding continuous learning into the strategic fabric of the organization, it becomes a fundamental aspect of its culture, driving ongoing improvement and enabling it to navigate the complexities and challenges of a rapidly changing world. This sustained commitment to learning and improvement will ultimately be the defining factor in an organization's long-term success and resilience.

Fostering Innovation and Creativity

Fostering a culture that actively encourages innovation and creativity is not simply a matter of installing a suggestion box; it requires a fundamental shift in how an organization operates, from its leadership style to its day-to-day processes. It's about cultivating an environment where innovative thinking is not just tolerated but celebrated, and where experimentation, even if it leads to failure, is seen as a valuable learning experience. This involves a multi-pronged approach that addresses structural impediments, leadership behavior, and the overall organizational mindset.

One of the most significant barriers to innovation is the fear of failure. Many organizations inadvertently create a culture where risk aversion reigns supreme. Employees are hesitant to propose unconventional ideas, fearing criticism or retribution for proposing something that might not work. To overcome this, organizations need to consciously cultivate a culture of psychological safety, where employees feel empowered to express their ideas without fear of judgment.

This starts at the top; leaders must model vulnerability, openly sharing their own mistakes and learning experiences. This sets a precedent for open communication and honest feedback, creating an environment where employees feel safe to take risks. Celebrating "intelligent failures" – those failures that resulted from thoughtful experimentation – is crucial. By focusing on the learning process and the effort invested, rather than solely on the outcome, organizations can encourage a growth mindset and reduce the fear associated with taking risks.

Open communication channels are essential for fostering innovation. This involves creating multiple avenues for employees to share their ideas, concerns, and suggestions. Regular brainstorming sessions, facilitated by trained professionals, can generate a wide range of ideas and stimulate creative thinking. These sessions should be designed to foster collaboration and encourage diverse perspectives. Open-door policies and informal communication channels, such as suggestion boxes or online forums, can also provide valuable avenues for gathering ideas and fostering a sense of ownership among employees. Moreover, actively soliciting feedback from customers and other stakeholders can provide invaluable insights into unmet needs and potential opportunities for innovation. The key is to create a system where information flows freely and is actively sought out, ensuring that a diverse range of voices are heard.

Collaboration is the engine of innovation. By encouraging cross-functional teams and breaking down organizational silos, organizations can foster the exchange of ideas and perspectives. Teams composed of individuals with different backgrounds, skills, and experiences can bring a wider range of perspectives to problem-solving, leading to more creative and effective solutions. This also means actively promoting interdepartmental communication and knowledge sharing. Tools like project management software can facilitate collaboration, ensuring that everyone is aware of the progress being made and can contribute their expertise. Regular team-building activities and social events can further strengthen relationships and enhance collaboration. The goal is to create a sense of community and shared purpose, where individuals feel empowered to work together towards a common goal.

Experimentation is the lifeblood of innovation. Organizations must create a safe space for employees to experiment with new ideas and approaches. This requires establishing processes for prototyping, testing, and iteratively improving upon ideas. A culture of experimentation accepts that not every idea will succeed; failure is seen as an integral part of the learning process. Organizations can establish dedicated "innovation labs" or "skunkworks" – separate units designed for experimentation– allowing employees to explore unconventional ideas without impacting core business operations. The key is to foster a culture where experimentation is valued, and individuals are not penalized for taking risks. A clear framework for assessing the outcome of experiments, focusing on the lessons learned, is also essential. This allows organizations to systematically learn from both successes and failures, iteratively improving their innovation process.

Incentivizing innovation is essential for its sustainability. This goes beyond monetary rewards; it encompasses recognizing and rewarding innovative contributions through formal and informal methods. Publicly acknowledging employees who have generated innovative ideas or implemented successful innovations fosters a sense of accomplishment and encourages others to follow suit. This recognition can take various forms – from simple verbal praise and team acknowledgements to more formal awards and promotions. Furthermore, creating dedicated career paths for individuals interested in innovation allows them to pursue their passions and contribute meaningfully to the organization's innovation efforts. This could involve creating specialist roles, providing access to advanced training, and establishing mentoring programs that facilitate knowledge transfer and career advancement within the innovation sector.

Learning from others is an integral part of fostering innovation. Benchmarking against industry leaders, attending industry conferences, and participating in professional networks can provide valuable insights into successful innovation strategies. Organizations can also benefit from collaborating with universities, research institutions, and external partners to gain access to cutting-edge knowledge and expertise. Regularly reviewing industry trends and best practices, and adapting them to the organization's specific needs, ensures that the organization remains at the forefront of innovation. This continuous learning process informs and shapes the organization's innovation strategies, ensuring they remain relevant and effective in a constantly evolving landscape.

Several companies have successfully implemented these strategies. Google, known for its culture of experimentation and employee empowerment, actively encourages employees to dedicate 20% of their time to pursuing personal projects. This has led to some of Google's most successful products and services. 3M, through its long-standing policy of allowing engineers to devote a portion of their time to personal projects, has fostered a culture of innovation, resulting in countless innovative products, including Post-it Notes.

Intuit, a financial software company, fosters a culture of innovation through its "Intuit Open Innovation" program, which actively seeks out and collaborates with external innovators. These examples demonstrate that fostering a culture of innovation is not simply a matter of chance but a strategic decision that requires a conscious and concerted effort.

By implementing these strategies, organizations can cultivate a culture of innovation that enables them to adapt to change, solve complex problems, and achieve sustained success in today's dynamic environment. The journey towards a truly innovative organization is an ongoing process, requiring consistent effort and a commitment to continuous learning and improvement. But the rewards – increased creativity, improved problem-solving capabilities, and enhanced competitiveness – are well worth the investment. Ultimately, fostering innovation is not just about generating new ideas; it's about transforming the organizational DNA to embrace a future where adaptation and creativity are not merely valued, but essential for survival and prosperity.

Empowering Employees and Decentralizing Decision Making

Empowering employees and decentralizing decision-making are not merely buzzwords in today's dynamic business landscape; they are fundamental pillars of adaptability. In an environment characterized by rapid change and unforeseen disruptions, organizations that cling to hierarchical structures and centralized control find themselves ill-equipped to respond effectively. Conversely, organizations that empower their employees and distribute decision-making authority create a nimble, responsive, and innovative workforce capable of navigating complexity and uncertainty with greater agility.

The core principle underlying this approach is trust. Trust in the capabilities and judgment of employees is paramount. Centralized decision-making often assumes that only senior management possesses the necessary knowledge and expertise to make sound judgments. However, this assumption overlooks the wealth of experience, insight, and creativity that resides within the organization at all levels. By distributing decision-making authority, organizations tap into this vast reservoir of talent, fostering a sense of shared responsibility and ownership.

Delegating authority effectively requires a clear understanding of the principles involved. It's not simply about passing down tasks; it's about entrusting employees with the autonomy to make decisions within defined parameters. This requires establishing clear expectations, providing the necessary resources and support, and fostering an environment of open communication and feedback. Clear guidelines and decision-making frameworks are essential to ensure consistency and alignment with organizational goals.

These frameworks should empower employees to make informed decisions while providing a safety net to prevent major deviations from strategy. Regular check-ins and performance reviews can provide valuable feedback and opportunities for adjustments, ensuring that the delegation process remains effective.

Fostering employee participation in the decision-making process is vital. This can take many forms, from soliciting input on strategic initiatives to involving employees in problem-solving and innovation efforts. Techniques like brainstorming sessions, focus groups, and suggestion boxes can provide valuable avenues for gathering employee feedback and ideas. Actively listening to and considering employee perspectives not only improves decision quality but also boosts morale and fosters a sense of ownership. Employees who feel their voices are heard are more likely to be engaged, motivated, and invested in the success of the organization. This increased engagement translates into greater adaptability and resilience during times of change.

Promoting a sense of ownership is another critical aspect of empowering employees. When employees feel a sense of ownership over their work and the organization's success, they are more likely to take initiative, be proactive in problem-solving, and actively seek out opportunities for improvement. This sense of ownership can be cultivated through various strategies, including providing employees with opportunities for professional development, involving them in strategic planning, and recognizing and rewarding their contributions. Transparency in communication is vital, ensuring that employees understand the organization's goals, challenges, and successes. This shared understanding fosters a sense of collective purpose and strengthens the bond between employees and the organization.

Overcoming challenges associated with decentralizing decision-making requires careful planning and execution. One common concern is the potential for inconsistencies in decision-making across different parts of the organization. To mitigate this risk, clear guidelines, standardized procedures, and regular communication are crucial. Training programs can equip employees with the skills and knowledge they need to make effective decisions.

A robust reporting and monitoring system can help identify potential inconsistencies and address them promptly. Another challenge lies in ensuring accountability. When decisions are decentralized, it's essential to establish clear lines of responsibility and ensure that employees are held accountable for their actions. This requires a system of checks and balances and a culture of transparency and open communication.

Several organizations have successfully decentralized decision-making, realizing significant benefits in terms of adaptability and innovation. For example, consider companies like Valve Corporation, known for its unique organizational structure, which eschews traditional hierarchical management. Employees work in self-organizing teams, with individuals choosing their projects and roles based on their interests and skills. This flat organizational structure promotes rapid response to market changes and fosters a highly innovative and adaptable culture. Similarly, companies like W.L. Gore & Associates, known for its innovative Gore-Tex fabric, empower employees through its "lattice organization," a structure that encourages collaboration and decentralized decision-making. This structure has fostered a culture of innovation and agility, enabling the company to adapt to changing market demands and technological advancements. These examples demonstrate that decentralized decision-making is not simply a theoretical ideal but a viable and effective strategy for fostering adaptability.

The impact of empowering employees and decentralizing decision-making extends beyond immediate operational efficiency. It fosters a culture of trust, collaboration, and innovation. Employees feel valued and respected, leading to increased job satisfaction and engagement. This, in turn, can lead to higher retention rates, reduced turnover costs, and improved overall organizational performance. The investment in empowering employees pays off not only in terms of adaptability but also in terms of building a strong, engaged, and high-performing workforce.

The transition to a more decentralized and empowering organizational structure is not a quick fix but a gradual process that requires careful planning and implementation. It involves a change in organizational culture, leadership style, and management practices. Leaders must embrace a more coaching and mentoring style, providing support and guidance to employees as they take on greater responsibility. They must also foster an environment of open communication, feedback, and trust. Training programs can equip employees with the necessary skills and knowledge to make effective decisions. Continuous improvement is key, with regular evaluation and adjustments to the process to ensure its effectiveness.

Ultimately, empowering employees and decentralizing decision-making are not simply about distributing authority; they are about fostering a culture of trust, collaboration, and shared responsibility. It's about recognizing the inherent talent and creativity within the organization and harnessing it to create a more agile, responsive, and innovative workforce. The journey requires commitment, patience, and a willingness to adapt and learn along the way. However, the benefits – increased adaptability, improved innovation, enhanced employee engagement, and stronger organizational performance – make the investment well worth the effort.

The successful implementation of these strategies lays a strong foundation for the enduring success and resilience of any organization in the face of ongoing and unpredictable change. It's not just about surviving; it's about thriving in a dynamic environment.

Measuring and Tracking Progress Towards Adaptability

Measuring and tracking progress toward a more adaptable organization isn't a simple task. It requires a multifaceted approach that combines quantitative data with qualitative insights. A purely numerical approach, while providing a sense of progress, risks overlooking the crucial nuances of human behavior and cultural shifts that underpin true adaptability. Therefore, a balanced strategy is essential, integrating hard data with observations of employee behavior and organizational responses to change.

One of the first steps is to define clear and measurable objectives. Instead of vague goals like "become more adaptable," we need concrete, actionable targets. These objectives should align directly with the organization's overall strategic goals and reflect the specific areas where adaptability is most crucial. For example, a company might aim to reduce its response time to market changes by 50% within a year or increase employee participation in innovation initiatives by 25%. These specific targets provide tangible benchmarks against which progress can be measured.

Key Performance Indicators (KPIs) are crucial for tracking progress. These KPIs should be selected carefully, reflecting the chosen objectives. While traditional KPIs such as revenue growth and market share remain important, new metrics directly addressing adaptability are needed. Consider metrics like:

Speed of response to market changes:
This could measure the time taken to introduce new products or services in response to market demands or competitive actions. The data could be drawn from the time elapsed between market signals and the implementation of corrective measures. A reduced response time indicates improved adaptability.

Employee engagement in change initiatives:
This metric assesses the level of participation and commitment employees demonstrate when organizational changes are implemented. Surveys, focus groups, and observation of participation in change management workshops can provide insights. Higher engagement suggests a stronger adaptive culture.

Innovation rate:
The number of new ideas generated, implemented, and successfully launched within a set period can reflect the organization's capacity for innovation and adaptability. This KPI necessitates a system for tracking and evaluating the success of innovative initiatives.

Resilience to disruptions:
This assesses the organization's ability to recover from

setbacks, whether internal (e.g., operational failures) or external (e.g., natural disasters, economic downturns). The speed and efficiency of recovery are key indicators of resilience and adaptability. Quantitative metrics can include recovery time, financial losses, and business continuity metrics.

Employee feedback on adaptability:
Regular employee surveys can gauge their perceptions of the organization's adaptability, its responsiveness to their suggestions, and the support they receive during periods of change. This qualitative data provides a crucial understanding of the human dimension of organizational adaptability.

Number of successful pivots:
This KPI tracks the number of successful strategic shifts the organization has made in response to changing market conditions, competitive pressures, or unforeseen circumstances. A high number of successful pivots showcases the organization's capacity to adapt.

Establishing benchmarks is crucial to measure the effectiveness of implemented strategies. These benchmarks can be based on internal historical data, industry averages, or best-in-class performers. By comparing the organization's performance to established benchmarks, progress can be objectively assessed. This allows for both internal comparisons (tracking improvements over time) and external comparisons (assessing the organization's position relative to competitors). Regular reporting on these KPIs, comparing progress against the established

benchmarks, provides a clear picture of progress and potential areas needing
attention.

The communication of progress is just as vital as the measurement itself. Regular reports, presented visually appealingly through dashboards and charts, should be disseminated to all stakeholders. This transparency builds trust, keeps employees informed, and fosters a shared sense of progress. The reports should not only focus on the quantitative data but also include narratives and qualitative insights that explain the data and highlight both successes and areas for improvement. For example, a company aiming to improve its response time to market changes could present a chart showing the reduction in response time over several quarters, alongside qualitative data explaining the strategies that led to these improvements. This holistic approach to communication ensures a comprehensive understanding of progress and fosters a culture of continuous improvement.

Implementing these measurements and tracking strategies requires the establishment of a robust data collection and analysis system. This system might involve a combination of existing enterprise resource planning (ERP) systems, specialized project management tools, and employee feedback mechanisms. Regular reviews of the data are critical, enabling adjustments to strategies as needed. The measurement system itself should be adaptive, evolving to reflect the organization's changing needs and priorities as it navigates its journey towards greater adaptability.

It's essential to acknowledge that building adaptability is an ongoing process, not a destination. The metrics and tracking mechanisms should be viewed as dynamic tools, regularly reviewed and refined to provide the most accurate and relevant picture of progress. The focus should not solely be on achieving numerical targets, but also on nurturing a culture where adaptability is deeply embedded in the organizational DNA. This involves fostering a growth mindset, encouraging continuous learning, and creating an environment where experimentation and risk-taking are rewarded.

Measuring and tracking progress towards a more adaptable organization demands a multi-pronged approach, combining quantitative data with qualitative insights. By selecting relevant KPIs, establishing clear benchmarks, and communicating progress transparently, organizations can effectively monitor their progress toward becoming more agile, resilient, and future-ready. The journey toward adaptability is not a sprint, but a marathon requiring continuous monitoring, adaptation, and a deep understanding of the interplay between data and organizational culture. The commitment to continuous improvement, reflected in the ongoing adaptation of the measurement strategies themselves, is the hallmark of a truly adaptable organization. It is this ongoing process of refinement, learning, and adaptation that will ultimately lead to lasting success.

Chapter 5: Leading Through Pivotal Moments

Recognizing and Responding to Pivotal Moments

Recognizing and responding effectively to pivotal moments is paramount for organizations aiming for sustained success in today's dynamic environment. These moments – critical junctures demanding decisive action and strategic shifts – can be the catalyst for either significant growth or devastating setbacks. The ability to identify these turning points early and respond with agility and precision is a hallmark of adaptive leadership.

One of the primary approaches to recognizing pivotal moments involves anticipating market shifts. This requires a proactive, almost anticipatory, stance, moving beyond simply reacting to immediate events. Effective leaders cultivate a deep understanding of market trends, competitive landscapes, and emerging technologies. They utilize a combination of market research, data analytics, and competitive intelligence to identify potential disruptions or opportunities well before they become fully manifest. This anticipatory approach allows for the development of proactive strategies, minimizing reactive measures and maximizing opportunities for strategic advantage.

For example, consider the rise of e-commerce. Companies that recognized the pivotal moment presented by the internet's increasing accessibility and consumer adoption early on, proactively invested in online platforms and adapted their business models accordingly, were able to thrive. Those who remained entrenched in traditional brick-and-mortar models, failing to recognize the shift, faced significant challenges and, in many cases, market irrelevance. This emphasizes the critical need for continuous monitoring of the external environment and a willingness to challenge existing assumptions.

Analyzing both internal and external data is equally vital in identifying pivotal moments. Internal data, such as sales figures, production efficiency, employee satisfaction surveys, and financial performance indicators, often reveals early warning signs of potential problems. A sharp decline in sales, a surge in production costs, or a drop in employee morale might signal the need for a strategic shift. External data, on the other hand, provides a broader context, encompassing market trends, competitor actions, technological advancements, and regulatory changes. By combining internal and external data analysis, a more comprehensive picture emerges, offering a clearer view of potential pivotal moments.

This integrated approach to data analysis requires sophisticated data management and analytical capabilities. Organizations need to invest in robust data infrastructure, capable of collecting, storing, and processing large volumes of both structured and unstructured data. Advanced analytical tools, such as machine learning and artificial intelligence, can be instrumental in identifying patterns and anomalies that might otherwise go unnoticed, offering early alerts of significant changes in the business environment. This proactive use of data, translating it into actionable insights, is crucial for effective response to pivotal moments.

Recognizing early warning signs of potential challenges or opportunities is a key skill for adaptive leaders. These signs are often subtle, requiring keen observation and critical thinking to decipher. They might manifest in shifts in customer behavior, changes in supplier relationships, emerging technological breakthroughs, or shifts in regulatory landscapes. Often, these signs are not immediately apparent and require actively seeking feedback from diverse sources, such as employees, customers, partners, and industry experts. The creation of a culture that encourages open communication and feedback sharing is essential for early identification of such warning signals.

Once a pivotal moment is identified, the next crucial step is assessing its impact. This requires a thorough understanding of the factors involved, their potential consequences, and the organization's resources and capabilities. Scenario planning can be a valuable tool in this assessment. By creating different scenarios, ranging from optimistic to pessimistic outcomes, organizations can better prepare for a range of possibilities and develop contingency plans. This approach helps avoid the paralysis of analysis, ensuring a proactive and informed response.

Determining the best course of action requires careful consideration of various factors. The chosen strategy must align with the organization's overall goals, resources, and risk tolerance. It must also be adaptable, allowing for adjustments as new information becomes available. This often involves balancing short-term needs with long-term strategic goals. A purely reactive approach, focused solely on immediate problems, might sacrifice long-term growth and sustainability. Conversely, a purely proactive approach, without sufficient consideration of short-term realities, could lead to unsustainable actions. The optimal strategy lies in finding the right balance between these two approaches.

Real-world examples illustrate the crucial role of effective response to pivotal moments. Consider the automotive industry's transformation in response to the rise of electric vehicles. Companies that recognized this pivotal moment and invested heavily in electric vehicle technology are now positioned for leadership in the new era of automotive manufacturing. Conversely, those who failed to recognize the shift or delayed their response are now struggling to catch up. The response to the COVID-19 pandemic also provides compelling examples. Organizations that quickly adapted their operations, embracing remote work and digital technologies, were better able to navigate the challenges and emerge stronger. Those that lagged behind suffered significant setbacks.

Recognizing and responding to pivotal moments is not just a desirable skill for leaders; it's a necessity for sustained success in a volatile and unpredictable world. By anticipating market shifts, analyzing internal and external data, recognizing early warning signs, assessing impact, and determining the appropriate course of action, organizations can effectively navigate crucial turning points, transforming challenges into opportunities. This requires a combination of proactive planning, adaptability, and a willingness to embrace change, transforming potential setbacks into stepping stones for future growth. The ability to effectively navigate these moments is a defining characteristic of truly adaptive and resilient organizations.

Developing this capability requires a culture of continuous learning, a commitment to data-driven decision making, and a willingness to challenge conventional thinking. The leaders who master this skill will be the ones who shape the future, not simply react to it.

Making Difficult Decisions Under Pressure

Making sound judgments during periods of intense pressure is a critical leadership skill, especially when navigating pivotal moments. These moments demand swift action, yet often involve incomplete information and significant uncertainty. The ability to make timely, informed decisions, even when facing ambiguity, separates effective leaders from those who falter under the weight of crisis. This requires a structured approach that balances speed with thoroughness, intuition with analysis.

One key strategy involves a rigorous risk assessment. This goes beyond simply identifying potential pitfalls; it requires a deep understanding of the probabilities and potential consequences of each outcome. This necessitates a systematic evaluation, considering both the upside and downside of various options. A useful framework is to create a decision matrix, listing potential choices along one axis and potential outcomes along another. Each cell in the matrix can then be populated with a quantitative assessment of the likelihood and impact of each outcome for each choice. This allows for a clear visualization of the risk-reward profile associated with each decision.

Quantifying risk, however, isn't always straightforward. Subjective judgments often play a role, especially in situations lacking historical data or clear precedents. In such cases, utilizing tools like sensitivity analysis can prove invaluable. Sensitivity analysis involves systematically varying the input parameters of the decision model to determine how sensitive the outcome is to changes in these parameters. This helps to identify which factors are most critical and which areas require further investigation or refinement. For example, when deciding on a new product launch, sensitivity analysis might examine the impact of varying assumptions about market size, production costs, or marketing effectiveness.

Managing uncertainty is another critical element. In many pivotal moments, the future is far from certain. Adopting a probabilistic approach is essential. Instead of focusing on a single, "best-case" scenario, leaders should consider a range of possibilities, acknowledging the inherent uncertainty. Scenario planning, as mentioned previously, is an effective tool for this. Developing multiple scenarios – best-case, worst-case, and several plausible alternatives – allows leaders to prepare for different contingencies and develop flexible plans that can adapt to changing circumstances.

This process isn't merely about predicting the future; it's about enhancing preparedness. Each scenario should prompt the identification of potential obstacles and the development of mitigation strategies. Regularly reviewing and updating these scenarios as new information emerges is crucial to maintaining adaptability. This iterative process allows for continuous adjustment of plans based on evolving circumstances, ensuring that the organization remains agile and responsive to unexpected events.

Effective decision-making under pressure requires overcoming cognitive biases, inherent mental shortcuts that can distort judgment. Confirmation bias, the tendency to seek out information that confirms pre-existing beliefs and ignore contradictory evidence, is particularly insidious. Leaders must consciously strive for objectivity, actively seeking out diverse perspectives and challenging their own assumptions. Anchoring bias, where decisions are heavily influenced by the first piece of information received, can also lead to poor choices. Techniques such as structured decision-making processes and the use of objective criteria can help mitigate this bias.

Another crucial element is the efficient processing of information. In high-pressure situations, the influx of data can be overwhelming. Leaders need to develop effective systems for filtering and prioritizing information, focusing on what's truly relevant and discarding unnecessary details. Data visualization techniques can be incredibly helpful in this process, presenting complex information in a clear and concise manner. This enables quicker comprehension and facilitates more informed decisions.

The importance of timely decisions cannot be overstated. Procrastination, while seemingly a safe option in the face of uncertainty, often leads to worse outcomes. Delayed decisions can allow problems to escalate, making them more difficult and costly to address. Establishing clear decision-making deadlines and sticking to them is crucial. This doesn't mean rushing into poorly considered choices; it emphasizes the importance of structured processes that allow for swift yet informed action.

Analyzing case studies of successful decision-making under pressure offers valuable insights. Consider the actions taken by companies during the 2008 financial crisis. Those who acted decisively, restructuring their operations and adapting to the changing market conditions, fared far better than those who delayed or failed to react appropriately. Similarly, companies that quickly pivoted during the COVID-19 pandemic, embracing remote work and adapting their supply chains, demonstrated the value of swift, decisive action. These examples highlight the critical role of adaptability and preparedness.

Effective leaders recognize the need to foster a culture that supports sound decision-making under pressure. This includes open communication, transparency, and the empowerment of teams. Encouraging open dialogue and sharing of information across different organizational levels creates a more informed and cohesive decision-making environment. Providing teams with the autonomy to make decisions within defined parameters empowers them and fosters a more resilient and responsive organization. This decentralized approach allows for quicker adaptation to changing circumstances, which is crucial during pivotal moments.

Finally, continuous learning and self-reflection are essential for improving decision-making capabilities. Leaders should actively seek out feedback on their decisions, both positive and negative, and analyze their successes and failures. This self-awareness, combined with a willingness to learn from mistakes, is vital for developing the resilience and adaptability needed to navigate the challenges of leading through pivotal moments. By constantly refining their approach, leaders can enhance their capacity for making effective decisions, even under the intense pressure of uncertainty and incomplete information. This continuous improvement process is not just a desirable trait; it's a necessity for those who aspire to lead effectively in today's volatile environment. The ability to navigate these moments decisively is not simply a skill; it's a defining characteristic of exceptional leadership.

Communicating Effectively During Times of Change

Effective communication is the lifeblood of any organization, but during periods of significant change, its importance is amplified exponentially. When facing pivotal moments, the way leaders communicate directly impacts employee morale, stakeholder confidence, and ultimately, the success of the transformation. A well-crafted communication strategy can transform uncertainty into opportunity, while poor communication can exacerbate anxieties and undermine even the most well-intentioned initiatives.

The first crucial aspect is timing and frequency. During times of change, information vacuums breed rumors and speculation, often far more damaging than the actual news. A consistent flow of information, even if it's just to acknowledge uncertainty, is far preferable to silence. Regular updates, delivered through multiple channels (email, town hall meetings, intranet posts), keep everyone informed and help manage expectations. The frequency should be appropriate to the situation; daily updates may be necessary during a crisis, while weekly updates might suffice for a more gradual transition. Leaders should resist the temptation to withhold information in the hope of avoiding negative reactions. Transparency, even when delivering difficult news, builds trust and fosters a more collaborative environment.

The content of communication is equally important. Clarity and conciseness are paramount. Avoid jargon and technical language that might confuse or alienate employees. Messages should be easily understood, focusing on the "what," "why," and "how" of the changes. The "what" explains the specific changes being implemented. The "why" provides the rationale behind these changes, linking them to the organization's overall goals and strategy. This context is crucial for gaining buy-in and minimizing resistance. The "how" details the implementation plan, outlining timelines, responsibilities, and potential impacts.

Visual aids can significantly enhance understanding. Charts, graphs, and infographics can transform complex data into easily digestible information. This is particularly helpful when communicating financial implications, restructuring plans, or technological upgrades. The use of visual aids also enhances engagement and helps retain key information. Visual communication can effectively communicate complex ideas to a wider audience, regardless of linguistic barriers.

Active listening is an equally vital component. Effective communication is a two-way street. Leaders must actively solicit feedback from employees at all levels. This can be achieved through various channels, including surveys, focus groups, suggestion boxes, and open forums. Creating safe spaces for employees to voice concerns, ask questions, and express anxieties is crucial. These spaces should be free of judgment, fostering an environment of open dialogue and mutual respect. Ignoring or dismissing concerns only serves to fuel anxiety and mistrust.

Different stakeholders require different communication approaches. Employees might need detailed information about their roles and responsibilities, whereas investors will be primarily interested in the financial implications of the change. Customers may need reassurance about the continued quality of products or services. Tailoring the message to the specific needs and interests of each stakeholder group ensures that the communication resonates and avoids causing unnecessary confusion or alarm. A multi-pronged approach is often the most effective, leveraging different communication channels to reach different audiences with customized messaging.

Handling difficult questions with grace and transparency is crucial. During times of change, employees may have legitimate anxieties about job security, workload increases, or the long-term impact of the changes. Leaders should avoid evasive answers or attempting to minimize concerns. Acknowledging the validity of their concerns, even when lacking definitive answers, fosters trust. Instead of providing immediate solutions, leaders can commit to exploring the issue further, providing updates as information becomes available. This approach demonstrates honesty and empathy, fostering a more positive and collaborative atmosphere. Maintaining morale during uncertainty is a challenge, but effective communication can play a significant role.

Celebrating small wins, acknowledging the efforts of employees, and emphasizing the shared vision can help maintain momentum and positivity. Regular communication reinforcing the positive impact of the changes and their benefits for the organization can bolster morale. Leadership's consistent optimism and confidence can be contagious, building resilience and fostering a sense of shared purpose. Recognition and rewards for employees who embrace the change can further incentivize participation and reduce resistance.

Beyond formal communication channels, informal communication can also play a vital role. Leaders should actively participate in informal interactions with employees, fostering a culture of open dialogue and accessibility. This allows for direct address of concerns and the quick clarification of misunderstandings. Informal communication can enhance transparency, fostering a feeling of connection and building trust amongst team members.

The use of storytelling can also greatly enhance communication during change. Narratives that link the current situation to the organization's history, values, and future aspirations can connect with employees on an emotional level, generating buy-in and promoting a sense of shared purpose. Stories that highlight examples of successful adaptations to previous challenges can build confidence and demonstrate resilience. These narratives are particularly powerful in conveying the overall vision and illustrating the positive outcomes anticipated from the change.

Throughout the entire communication process, consistency and authenticity are paramount. Messages should be consistent across all platforms and channels, ensuring that all stakeholders receive the same information. Leaders must also communicate authentically, being genuine in their expressions of concern and optimism. Transparency and consistency in communication build trust and confidence, which is especially important during times of change. Inconsistent messages or a perceived lack of authenticity will quickly erode the trust that's crucial for effective change management.

Effective communication during periods of significant change is an iterative process. Leaders should continually monitor employee feedback and adjust their communication strategy accordingly. This may involve altering the frequency of updates, adjusting the messaging, or changing communication channels to reach a wider audience. Continuous monitoring and adaptation ensure that communication remains relevant, effective, and responsive to the evolving needs of the organization and its stakeholders. This ongoing process of assessment and refinement is key to managing change successfully.

Managing Resistance and Maintaining Momentum

Managing resistance is an inevitable aspect of leading through pivotal moments. Change, even when positive and necessary, often triggers anxieties and uncertainties within an organization. Addressing these concerns proactively and constructively is vital for maintaining momentum and ensuring a successful transition. Ignoring resistance, hoping it will simply dissipate, is a recipe for disaster; it fosters resentment, undermines morale, and can ultimately derail the entire change initiative.

One of the most effective strategies for managing resistance is to understand its root causes. Resistance isn't always about outright opposition; it often stems from fear of the unknown, concerns about job security, perceived loss of control, or a lack of understanding about the rationale behind the changes. Through open communication, active listening, and empathetic engagement, leaders can uncover these underlying anxieties and address them effectively. This requires more than just delivering information; it demands a genuine effort to understand the perspectives and concerns of individuals and teams.

Building trust and transparency is paramount. Employees are more likely to embrace change when they trust their leaders and feel confident in the process. This trust is built through consistent communication, honest dialogue, and a demonstrated commitment to fairness and equity. Transparency is crucial—employees need to understand the "why" behind the changes, the potential benefits, and the plan for implementation. When leaders are open and honest, even about uncertainties, they foster a culture of trust and collaboration. Conversely, withholding information or attempting to control the narrative fuels suspicion and resistance.

Active listening goes beyond simply hearing; it involves genuinely engaging with employees' concerns, validating their feelings, and demonstrating empathy. Creating forums for open dialogue, whether through town hall meetings, focus groups, or one-on-one conversations, allows employees to express their anxieties and ask questions. Leaders should actively solicit feedback and demonstrate a willingness to address concerns, even if they don't have all the answers. This willingness to listen and engage demonstrates respect and builds a sense of shared ownership in the change process.

Addressing resistance effectively often involves managing conflict constructively. Disagreements and tensions are inevitable during periods of change. The key is to approach these conflicts as opportunities for dialogue and problem-solving, not as battles to be won or lost. Leaders should create a safe space for expressing dissenting opinions, encouraging respectful debate, and fostering collaborative solutions. This requires strong facilitation skills, the ability to mediate disagreements, and a commitment to finding common ground.

Building consensus is another critical aspect of managing resistance. While it's impossible to achieve unanimous agreement on every aspect of change, striving for consensus helps build buy-in and minimizes resistance. This involves actively engaging with stakeholders, soliciting their input, and incorporating their ideas wherever possible. The process of collaboration itself can significantly reduce resistance, as individuals feel involved and valued. It demonstrates a commitment to inclusivity and acknowledges the importance of their contributions.

Motivating teams to embrace change requires a multi-faceted approach. One effective strategy is to emphasize the positive aspects of the change, highlighting the benefits for both the organization and individuals. This involves clearly articulating the vision for the future, the opportunities for growth and development, and the positive impact on the organization's success. Leaders can also use storytelling to connect with employees on an emotional level, sharing narratives that illustrate the significance of the change and its potential benefits.

Incentivizing participation is another powerful motivator. This might involve offering training and development opportunities, providing recognition and rewards for employees who embrace the change, or offering incentives for early adoption. Leaders should celebrate small wins along the way, reinforcing positive progress and building momentum. This positive reinforcement is crucial for maintaining morale and encouraging continued participation.

Overcoming resistance requires a comprehensive strategy that addresses both the practical and emotional aspects of change. This might involve providing adequate training and support, offering resources to help employees adapt, and creating a culture of continuous learning and development. Effective change management involves a proactive and ongoing process of communication, engagement, and support.

Consider the example of a company undergoing a digital transformation. Resistance might arise from employees concerned about the need to learn new technologies, potential job displacement, or increased workload. By providing comprehensive training programs, emphasizing the long-term benefits of the transformation (e.g., increased efficiency, new skill development), and addressing concerns about job security proactively, leaders can mitigate resistance and build buy-in. Open forums for employees to share their anxieties and ask questions, combined with regular updates on the progress of the transformation, are critical elements of this process.

Another example might be a company restructuring its operations. Resistance could arise from employees concerned about potential layoffs, changes in reporting structures, or the loss of established working relationships. In this scenario, leaders need to communicate transparently about the restructuring plans, explaining the rationale, outlining the timeline, and addressing concerns about job security. Retaining employees through re-skilling programs, and re-training can be a key part of this strategy.

Maintaining momentum throughout the change process is crucial for success. Regular progress updates, celebrating milestones, and acknowledging employee contributions help sustain engagement and keep the team focused on the desired outcome. Leaders should consistently reinforce the vision for the future, reminding employees of the positive impact of the changes and their role in achieving the organization's goals. A strong sense of shared purpose is essential for maintaining momentum and overcoming challenges.

Regularly assessing the effectiveness of change management strategies is also important. Leaders should monitor employee feedback, track progress towards goals, and make adjustments as needed. This might involve modifying communication strategies, addressing persistent resistance through targeted interventions, or providing additional support to struggling teams. A flexible and adaptive approach is essential for navigating the complexities of organizational change.

Managing resistance and maintaining momentum during pivotal moments requires a combination of strategic planning, effective communication, strong leadership, and a genuine commitment to employee well-being. By understanding the root causes of resistance, building trust and transparency, actively listening to concerns, and fostering collaboration, leaders can navigate even the most challenging transitions successfully. The consistent application of these principles, combined with a proactive and adaptable approach, ensures that the organization not only survives but thrives through periods of significant change. Organizations that can effectively manage change, fostering a culture of adaptability and resilience, are better positioned for success in the long term.

Learning from Pivotal Moments and Refining Strategies

Learning from past experiences is not merely an exercise in self-reflection; it's a critical component of developing robust and adaptable leadership. Pivotal moments, whether they result in resounding success or significant setbacks, offer invaluable opportunities for growth and refinement. To effectively leverage these experiences, a structured approach to post-event analysis is essential. This process goes beyond simple blame assignment or celebratory self-congratulation; it delves into the intricacies of the situation, identifying both successes and failures to inform future strategies.

A comprehensive post-event analysis typically involves several key steps. Firstly, a dedicated team should be assembled, bringing together individuals with diverse perspectives and expertise. This team should include members directly involved in the pivotal moment, as well as those with a broader organizational perspective. This diversity ensures a holistic evaluation, avoiding biases and blind spots that might otherwise emerge.

Next, the team needs to gather comprehensive data. This involves collecting information from various sources, including meeting minutes, internal communications, performance metrics, and even anecdotal accounts from employees at all levels. Analyzing financial reports, customer feedback, and market data can provide crucial contextual information, helping to illuminate the broader impact of the event. This data collection process should be thorough and meticulous, aiming to create a detailed and accurate record of the event's unfolding.

Once the data is gathered, the team should systematically analyze it. This involves identifying critical incidents, key decisions, and their respective outcomes. It's crucial to distinguish between cause and effect, avoiding simplistic conclusions and instead exploring the intricate interplay of various factors. For example, a successful product launch might be attributed to a brilliant marketing campaign, but a thorough analysis might reveal the critical role played by effective cross-functional collaboration or timely adaptation to changing market conditions. Equally, examining failures necessitates separating contributing factors from direct causes. A failed product launch might appear due to poor marketing, but the root cause might lie in a flawed product design or insufficient market research.

A critical element of this analysis is identifying lessons learned. These aren't simply statements of what went wrong or right; rather, they are actionable insights that can directly inform future strategies. For instance, recognizing that a lack of clear communication hampered a specific initiative might translate into a lesson to prioritize transparency and consistent updates in future projects. Similarly, a successful innovation might highlight the importance of fostering a culture of experimentation and risk-taking. These lessons should be clearly articulated, concrete, and readily applicable to future situations.

The identified lessons learned should then be integrated into a revised leadership strategy. This requires translating abstract insights into concrete actions. It involves creating specific, measurable, achievable, relevant, and time-bound (SMART) goals to guide future actions. For example, the lesson about communication might translate into a goal of implementing a weekly cross-functional communication meeting, with measurable progress tracked through participation rates and feedback surveys.

Incorporating these lessons into future strategies also requires updating relevant organizational processes and systems. This might involve modifying communication protocols, streamlining decision-making processes, or introducing new training programs to enhance specific skills. The goal is to build a more resilient and adaptable organization, better equipped to handle future pivotal moments. This proactive approach avoids reacting to challenges in an ad-hoc manner, instead establishing a structured framework for continuous improvement.

Creating a continuous improvement cycle is essential for sustained organizational learning. This involves regularly evaluating performance, identifying areas for improvement, and implementing changes. This cycle isn't a linear process; rather, it's an iterative one, with ongoing monitoring and adjustments based on feedback and evolving circumstances.

Establishing a culture of continuous learning fosters adaptability and resilience, enabling the organization to remain dynamic and responsive to change. This cycle should be embedded in the organization's culture, with regular opportunities for feedback and reflection. This could involve regular team retrospectives, formal performance reviews, or informal channels for sharing lessons learned. By creating a culture of open communication and mutual learning, organizations can foster a climate where mistakes are seen as opportunities for growth, rather than something to be hidden or avoided. Leadership should actively encourage this culture, recognizing and rewarding both successes and the lessons gleaned from setbacks.

Several organizations exemplify the power of learning from past pivotal moments. Consider the case of a major airline that successfully navigated a near-catastrophic safety incident. The ensuing investigation didn't simply identify immediate causes but also looked into underlying systemic issues. This led to sweeping changes in safety protocols, training programs, and maintenance procedures, significantly enhancing safety standards across the entire industry. The airline didn't just recover; it emerged stronger and more resilient, transforming a crisis into a catalyst for significant improvement.

Similarly, many technology companies have faced significant product failures, yet they've used these setbacks as launchpads for innovation. By thoroughly analyzing what went wrong, understanding user feedback, and adapting their strategies, they've often transformed failed products into successful iterations. This iterative approach to innovation demonstrates the power of learning from mistakes and using them to improve future outcomes. This proactive adaptation distinguishes successful organizations from those that stagnate in the face of setbacks.

Numerous organizations have demonstrated the importance of continuous improvement by establishing formal processes for post-event analysis and incorporating lessons learned into their overall strategy. From manufacturing firms striving for leaner operations to healthcare providers focused on patient safety, the commitment to continuous improvement is a hallmark of organizations that thrive in dynamic environments. These organizations leverage data analysis, feedback mechanisms, and internal communication strategies to foster a culture of continuous learning and adaptation. They consistently reflect on past experiences, learn from both successes and failures, and use those insights to enhance their effectiveness and resilience. This commitment to learning and adaptation ensures they remain ahead of the curve and capable of weathering any storm.

Effective leadership is not about avoiding setbacks; it's about successfully navigating them and leveraging those experiences to build a stronger, more resilient organization. By embracing a structured approach to post-event analysis, incorporating lessons learned, and fostering a culture of continuous improvement, leaders can transform pivotal moments from potential crises into opportunities for substantial organizational growth and enduring success. The proactive and iterative application of these principles distinguishes high-performing organizations from those that simply react to change rather than anticipate it. Building this capability requires a commitment to continuous learning, both at the individual and organizational level. It's a critical component of building future-ready leadership and organizations that thrive in today's rapidly changing world.

Chapter 6: Building High-Performing Adaptive Teams

Understanding Team Dynamics and Collaboration

Building high-performing, adaptive teams hinges on a deep understanding of team dynamics and the art of collaboration. It's more than simply assembling a group of skilled individuals; it's about fostering a cohesive unit that operates synergistically, leveraging individual strengths to achieve shared objectives. This requires careful consideration of several key elements, starting with the foundation of trust.

Trust, the bedrock of any successful team, isn't automatically bestowed; it's earned through consistent actions and behaviors. Team members need to feel confident that their colleagues are reliable, competent, and have their best interests at heart. This requires open and honest communication, where vulnerabilities are embraced rather than shunned, and disagreements are approached constructively, focusing on solutions rather than blame.

Leaders play a vital role in cultivating this trust, modeling transparency, accountability, and empathy. They must demonstrate a willingness to listen actively, consider diverse perspectives, and create a safe space for open dialogue, even when discussing challenging issues. This trust-building process is iterative and requires consistent effort, but the rewards are immense, leading to increased collaboration, improved decision-making, and a more engaged and productive team.

Effective communication is intrinsically linked to trust. It's not merely about the exchange of information; it's about ensuring that information is clearly understood, accurately interpreted, and acted upon. This requires clarity in conveying messages, active listening to ensure comprehension, and seeking continuous feedback. The choice of communication channels is also critical; some situations may warrant formal meetings, while others benefit from informal discussions or digital platforms. High- performing teams adapt their communication methods based on the context, recognizing that a rigid approach can stifle creativity and collaboration. For example, a brainstorming session might benefit from a more relaxed, informal setting, while a project update necessitates a clear, structured presentation. The key is flexibility and a commitment to ensuring that everyone feels heard and understood.

Shared goals provide a unifying focus for the team, aligning individual efforts towards a common purpose. This doesn't mean eliminating individual contributions; rather, it ensures that each member understands how their work contributes to the bigger picture. Clearly defined goals, communicated transparently and regularly reviewed, provide a sense of direction and motivation. They also facilitate effective performance management, allowing for regular tracking of progress and timely adjustments to strategy as needed. Without clearly defined goals, a team can easily become fragmented, with individual efforts pulling in different directions, leading to wasted resources and diminished overall effectiveness. The process of establishing these shared goals should be collaborative, involving input from all team members, ensuring ownership and commitment.

Mutual support is crucial for navigating challenges and fostering a positive team environment. High-performing teams recognize that setbacks are inevitable; however, they approach these challenges with a spirit of collective responsibility, providing support and encouragement to each other. This involves actively celebrating successes, offering constructive feedback during difficulties, and stepping in to help colleagues when needed. This kind of mutual support builds resilience within the team, enabling them to cope with pressure and overcome obstacles effectively. It creates a culture of psychological safety, where team members feel comfortable seeking help or admitting mistakes without fear of judgment or reprimand. Leaders play a key role in modeling this behavior, actively demonstrating support for their team members and fostering a culture of mutual respect and assistance.

Team structure significantly impacts team effectiveness. Different structures are suited to different tasks and organizational contexts. A hierarchical structure, with clear lines of authority, might be appropriate for complex projects requiring strict oversight, while a flat, decentralized structure could foster greater creativity and collaboration in more agile environments. Some teams benefit from a matrix structure, allowing individuals to report to multiple managers, enabling expertise sharing and cross-functional collaboration. High-performing teams demonstrate the ability to adapt their structure as needed, recognizing that a rigid structure can become a constraint when faced with dynamic situations. Regularly reviewing the team's structure, assessing its effectiveness, and making necessary adjustments are critical aspects of maintaining optimal performance. This adaptability ensures that the team can maintain agility and respond effectively to changing circumstances.

The ability to adapt processes is equally crucial. High-performing teams don't rigidly adhere to predefined procedures; instead, they continuously evaluate their workflows, identifying bottlenecks and inefficiencies. They are proactive in experimenting with different processes, adopting best practices, and making iterative improvements. This involves actively seeking feedback from team members, incorporating their suggestions, and utilizing data-driven approaches to assess the impact of process changes. This iterative process ensures that the team continuously optimizes its performance, remaining adaptable and responsive to changing demands. Leaders should actively support and encourage this process, providing the necessary resources and creating a culture that values experimentation and continuous improvement.

Examples of high-performing, adaptive teams abound across various sectors. Consider a software development team that utilizes agile methodologies. Their iterative approach, embracing change and incorporating user feedback throughout the development process, allows them to rapidly adapt to evolving requirements and deliver high-quality products. In contrast, a crisis management team within a hospital, responding to a sudden surge in patient volume during a public health emergency, showcases adaptability through swift adjustments to protocols and efficient resource allocation. Similarly, a marketing team launching a new product in a volatile market must quickly adapt their strategies based on market research and customer feedback.

These examples illustrate how high-performing teams, regardless of their industry, share common traits: a clear understanding of their goals, robust communication strategies, a culture of trust and mutual support, and the capacity to adapt both their structure and processes as needed.

Building high-performing, adaptive teams is a continuous process that requires conscious effort and a commitment to fostering a collaborative and supportive environment. It involves creating a culture of trust, establishing clear goals, ensuring effective communication, promoting mutual support, and embracing the ability to adapt both structure and processes. By understanding these key elements and consistently working to refine them, organizations can create teams that not only achieve remarkable results but also thrive. The key is not to strive for perfection, but for continuous improvement, learning from successes and failures, and adapting strategically to meet evolving challenges. The organizations that excel are those that embrace this dynamic, iterative approach to team building, fostering a culture of continuous learning and adaptability, ultimately leading to sustained organizational success.

Delegation and Empowerment in Adaptive Teams

Delegation and empowerment are not merely management techniques; they are fundamental pillars upon which high-performing adaptive teams are built. Clinging to a centralized, top-down approach is a recipe for stagnation. Adaptive teams thrive on distributed decision-making, fostering a culture where every member feels empowered to contribute their unique skills and perspectives. This requires a strategic shift in leadership thinking, moving away from a mindset of control towards one of trust and support.

Effective delegation begins with clarity. Ambiguity is the enemy of empowerment. Before assigning a task, leaders must meticulously define the desired outcome, outlining specific deliverables, timelines, and key performance indicators (KPIs). This clarity ensures everyone is on the same page, minimizing misunderstandings and avoiding wasted effort. The delegation process should incorporate a thorough assessment of the individual team member's skills and experience. Assigning tasks that align with an individual's strengths leverages their capabilities and fosters a sense of accomplishment, building confidence and increasing motivation.

Beyond defining the task, successful delegation involves providing the necessary resources and support. This goes beyond simply allocating budget or tools; it includes providing access to relevant information, mentorship, and guidance. Empowered team members are not left to fend for themselves; they have access to the knowledge and expertise they need to succeed. This may involve connecting them with mentors, providing access to training resources, or facilitating collaborative sessions with other team members possessing complementary skills. Leaders should proactively identify potential roadblocks and proactively address them, ensuring team members have the support they need to navigate challenges effectively.

Accountability is the counterpoint to empowerment. While granting autonomy is crucial, it's equally important to establish clear accountability mechanisms. This doesn't equate to micromanagement; rather, it involves creating a framework for regular progress updates, performance reviews, and constructive feedback. Open communication channels are essential, ensuring that team members can readily report challenges and seek assistance without fear of retribution. Regular check-ins, not for the purpose of controlling but for the purpose of supporting and guiding, allow leaders to provide timely assistance and address any emerging roadblocks before they escalate into significant problems.

Fostering a culture of trust is paramount. Empowerment cannot flourish in an environment of suspicion or distrust. Leaders must model trust by giving team members the benefit of the doubt, allowing them the freedom to experiment and learn from mistakes. A culture of psychological safety is essential, where team members feel comfortable taking risks and expressing dissenting opinions without fear of judgment or reprisal. This requires a conscious effort from leaders to cultivate a supportive and inclusive environment where mistakes are viewed as learning opportunities rather than failures.

Effective delegation in adaptive teams also involves embracing a distributed leadership model. This doesn't mean abandoning leadership; it means sharing leadership responsibilities across the team. Different individuals may emerge as leaders in different contexts, leveraging their expertise and influence to drive specific aspects of the project forward. This distributed approach leverages the collective intelligence of the team, accelerating decision-making and fostering a sense of shared ownership.

Consider the example of a product development team in a rapidly evolving tech startup. A traditional, hierarchical structure would likely stifle innovation and responsiveness.

Instead, an adaptive team structure might empower individual developers to own specific features or modules, delegating responsibility for design, coding, testing, and deployment. Regular sprint reviews and stand-up meetings ensure transparency and collaboration, allowing the team to adapt quickly to changing market demands or technological advancements. The project manager in this scenario acts as a facilitator, providing resources and guidance, rather than a central decision-maker. This distributed leadership model allows the team to respond swiftly to challenges, optimizing efficiency and accelerating product development.

Another illustration is a crisis management team in a hospital responding to a major emergency. In this high-pressure environment, clear delegation is not only efficient but potentially life-saving. The team leader might delegate specific roles based on individual expertise – for example, assigning a physician to oversee patient triage, a nurse to manage medication distribution, and a logistics specialist to handle resource allocation. Effective communication and clear lines of accountability are paramount. In such circumstances, empowering individuals to act decisively within their delegated responsibilities is critical, reducing response times and optimizing the use of limited resources.

Regular briefings and debriefings allow for collaborative problem-solving and continuous learning from the experience. The implementation of delegation and empowerment requires a conscious shift in leadership style. Leaders must relinquish some control, embracing a more facilitative approach. This requires a willingness to trust team members, to provide support without micromanaging, and to embrace experimentation and learning from failures. The benefits, however, are substantial. Empowered team members are more engaged, more motivated, and more likely to take ownership of their work. This leads to increased innovation, improved decision-making, and ultimately, greater organizational success.

However, delegation is not a one-size-fits-all solution. The appropriate level of delegation will vary depending on several factors, including the team's maturity, the complexity of the task, and the individual skills and experience of team members. For a newly formed team, a more structured approach with closer supervision may be necessary initially, gradually transitioning to greater autonomy as trust and competence develop. Conversely, a highly experienced and self-managing team may require minimal oversight, allowing for maximum flexibility and creativity. Leaders must adapt their delegation style accordingly, recognizing the need for a dynamic and adaptable approach.

Successful delegation also requires consistent feedback and recognition. Regular performance reviews, providing both constructive criticism and positive reinforcement, are vital for maintaining motivation and ensuring continuous improvement. Celebrating successes and acknowledging individual contributions fosters a sense of accomplishment and encourages further commitment. Publicly recognizing achievements further strengthens the team's collective sense of accomplishment and builds trust among members.

Finally, remember that delegation is a continuous process of learning and refinement. What works for one team or task might not be effective for another. Regular evaluation of delegation strategies, seeking feedback from team members, and adapting approaches as needed, ensures ongoing effectiveness. The goal is to build a culture of empowerment where every team member feels valued, respected, and empowered to contribute their best work, fostering a high-performing, adaptive team capable of navigating complexity and achieving remarkable results. This ongoing adaptation and refinement are what truly distinguish high-performing adaptive teams from their less effective counterparts.

Fostering Open Communication and Feedback Loops

Open communication isn't merely a desirable attribute in a high-performing adaptive team; it's the lifeblood that sustains its agility and resilience. Without the free flow of information, ideas, and concerns, a team quickly becomes siloed, its responses sluggish and its innovation stifled. Building a culture of open dialogue requires a conscious and consistent effort from leadership, demanding a shift away from traditional hierarchical structures towards a more collaborative and transparent environment.

One of the first steps towards fostering open communication is establishing clear and easily accessible channels for information exchange. This goes beyond simple email chains or infrequent meetings. Consider implementing a centralized communication platform, such as a project management software that incorporates task management, real-time messaging, and document sharing. Such platforms provide a single source of truth, minimizing the risk of miscommunication or missed information. Regular team meetings, whether daily stand-ups or weekly progress reviews, provide opportunities for open discussion, allowing team members to share updates, raise concerns, and brainstorm solutions collaboratively. These meetings should be structured to encourage participation from all members, with clear ground rules established to ensure respectful and productive dialogue. The use of visual management tools, such as Kanban boards or progress charts, can enhance transparency and allow team members to track progress and identify potential bottlenecks in real-time.

Actively cultivating a culture of active listening is paramount. This isn't merely about hearing what others say, it's about genuinely understanding their perspectives, empathizing with their concerns, and responding thoughtfully and respectfully. Leaders should model this behavior, demonstrating a commitment to active listening in all their interactions. Training sessions on active listening techniques, focusing on elements like paraphrasing, summarizing, and asking clarifying questions, can significantly enhance communication effectiveness within the team. Establishing a safe space where individuals feel comfortable expressing their thoughts and opinions, even if they differ from the majority view, is crucial. This requires a conscious effort to create a culture of psychological safety, where dissenting opinions are welcomed as opportunities for learning and improvement rather than as challenges to authority.

Beyond the tools and techniques, the tone and style of communication significantly influence its effectiveness. Leaders must set the tone by modeling respectful, open, and constructive communication. This includes being receptive to feedback, both positive and negative, and actively seeking out diverse perspectives. Promoting empathy and understanding, recognizing that individuals have different communication styles and preferences, is crucial. Leaders should strive to be approachable and accessible, creating an environment where team members feel comfortable sharing their ideas, concerns, and feedback without fear of judgment or reprisal. Open-door policies, where team members can easily approach leaders with questions or concerns, foster a sense of trust and transparency.

However, simply establishing communication channels isn't enough. To truly maximize the effectiveness of communication within an adaptive team, robust feedback loops are essential. These loops allow for continuous monitoring, evaluation, and adjustment of processes, strategies, and individual performance. Feedback should be a two-way street, flowing freely between team members, leaders, and stakeholders. Regular performance reviews should be a structured process, focused on open dialogue and mutual understanding rather than a top-down evaluation.

These reviews should not simply assess past performance but also look towards future goals and development plans. Constructive criticism, offered with empathy and a focus on improvement, is crucial for fostering individual growth and team effectiveness. 360-degree feedback mechanisms, where individuals receive feedback from multiple sources, including peers, subordinates, and supervisors, can provide a more holistic and accurate assessment of performance.

The implementation of these feedback loops requires careful planning and execution. Leaders should establish clear guidelines for providing and receiving feedback, emphasizing the importance of constructive language, specific examples, and actionable recommendations. Regular feedback sessions, integrated into the team's workflow, ensure that feedback is timely and relevant, allowing for swift adjustments and minimizing potential negative impacts. The use of feedback tools and surveys, both formal and informal, can help gather valuable insights and ensure that feedback reaches the appropriate individuals and channels. Regularly analyzing the feedback received and making adjustments to processes or strategies based on this feedback is crucial for continuous improvement.

Effective feedback loops are not solely about formal reviews and assessments; they should be integrated into the team's daily operations. Regular check-ins, team brainstorming sessions, and informal conversations provide opportunities for ongoing feedback and collaborative problem-solving. Celebrating successes and acknowledging individual contributions also forms a vital part of the feedback loop. Positive reinforcement and public recognition of accomplishments enhance morale, boost motivation, and strengthen the team's collective sense of achievement.

To illustrate the power of effective communication and feedback loops, consider the example of a software development team utilizing Agile methodologies. Daily stand-up meetings, sprint reviews, and retrospectives form the backbone of their communication and feedback processes. Through these regular interactions, the team swiftly identifies and addresses obstacles, shares progress updates, and proactively adapts to changing requirements. The retrospective meetings, in particular, offer a structured opportunity for the team to reflect on past sprints, identify areas for improvement in their processes and workflows, and collaboratively develop solutions. This continuous cycle of feedback and adaptation is a defining characteristic of high-performing Agile teams.

Another example can be found in a marketing team facing a sudden downturn in sales. Through open communication channels and transparent data sharing, the team quickly identifies the potential causes, such as a change in market trends or a flaw in their marketing strategy. By actively seeking feedback from customers through surveys and social media monitoring, and internally through brainstorming sessions, the team identifies potential solutions, refines their strategy, and implements necessary adjustments. This iterative process of feedback, analysis, and adaptation allows the team to rapidly respond to the challenge and reverse the negative trend.

In contrast, organizations that fail to establish effective communication and feedback loops often struggle with poor coordination, low morale, and a lack of responsiveness to change. Siloed teams, hindered by poor communication, frequently work in isolation, leading to duplication of efforts, missed deadlines, and a lack of innovation. The absence of constructive feedback mechanisms inhibits individual growth and team improvement, leading to stagnation and decreased productivity. This demonstrates that the implementation of open communication and robust feedback loops is not merely a nice-to-have but a critical success factor for any high-performing adaptive team navigating the complexities of today's dynamic business environment. The continuous flow of information, the constant exchange of ideas, and the proactive seeking and implementation of feedback are essential ingredients for building a team that is not only resilient but also highly responsive, innovative, and ultimately, successful. The journey towards creating this type of team requires commitment, consistent effort, and a willingness to adapt and evolve as the team matures and the business landscape shifts. It is a continuous process of learning, improvement, and adaptation that will ultimately lead to long-term success.

Managing Conflict and Disputes in Adaptive Teams

Conflict is inevitable in any team, but in adaptive teams, its management becomes even more critical. The very nature of adaptation—embracing change, experimenting with new approaches, and navigating uncertainty—creates fertile ground for disagreements. However, rather than viewing conflict as a negative force, high-performing adaptive teams recognize it as an opportunity for growth, innovation, and strengthened relationships. The key lies not in avoiding conflict, but in mastering the art of constructive conflict resolution.

The first step in effective conflict management is proactive identification. Waiting for conflict to escalate before addressing it is a recipe for disaster. Adaptive teams cultivate a culture of open communication where team members feel comfortable voicing concerns, even minor disagreements, before they fester into significant problems. Regular check-ins, facilitated by the team leader or a designated facilitator, provide a structured opportunity for individuals to express their thoughts and concerns without fear of reprisal. These check-ins aren't about problem-solving immediately; they're about early detection, creating a space for team members to articulate their perspectives, and for leaders to understand potential brewing conflicts. Active listening, as previously discussed, is vital at this stage. It's not enough to hear the words; leaders need to understand the underlying emotions and concerns that fuel the disagreements.

Once a conflict is identified, the next step is to understand its root causes. Often, the surface-level issue is just a symptom of a deeper underlying problem. For instance, a disagreement over project priorities might stem from unclear roles and responsibilities, a lack of shared vision, or inadequate communication. A team struggling with conflict needs to look beneath the surface to identify these root causes. Techniques like root cause analysis, often utilized in quality management systems, can help teams systematically identify the underlying issues driving the conflict. This process involves asking "why" repeatedly until the fundamental cause of the disagreement is uncovered. For example, if the conflict is about missed deadlines, asking "why" repeatedly might reveal issues with resource allocation, unrealistic timelines, or a lack of clear communication regarding dependencies between tasks.

Addressing the root causes is crucial because superficial solutions often fail to resolve the conflict permanently. If the root cause isn't addressed, the conflict is likely to re-emerge in different forms. Focusing on the symptoms, such as simply assigning blame or imposing a solution without addressing the underlying issues, only provides temporary relief. A truly effective resolution requires a collaborative approach, where team members work together to identify the root causes, brainstorm solutions, and agree upon an action plan.

Facilitating productive discussions is critical during the conflict resolution process. The team leader or facilitator should guide the discussion, ensuring that all team members have an opportunity to express their perspectives and concerns. It's important to establish ground rules for respectful dialogue, focusing on the issues at hand and avoiding personal attacks. Techniques such as active listening, paraphrasing to ensure understanding, and summarizing key points can help to keep the discussion focused and productive. Creating a safe space, where individuals feel comfortable expressing their viewpoints without fear of judgment, is paramount. This might involve explicitly stating that disagreements are expected and valued, that diverse perspectives are essential for innovation, and that constructive criticism is encouraged.

One particularly helpful technique is the use of structured brainstorming sessions. These sessions provide a framework for generating a wide range of potential solutions to the conflict. By encouraging participation from all team members, a more comprehensive range of solutions can be generated, increasing the likelihood of finding a solution that is acceptable to everyone involved. The team should focus on exploring multiple options, evaluating their feasibility, and prioritizing solutions based on their potential effectiveness and impact.

Reaching mutually acceptable solutions is the ultimate goal of conflict resolution. This doesn't necessarily mean that every individual gets exactly what they want; rather, it means that a solution is found that addresses the concerns of all parties involved and balances their needs. Compromise is often necessary, but it should not be at the expense of the team's overall goals and objectives. Collaborative problem-solving, where team members work together to create a solution that respects everyone's needs, is often a more effective approach than imposing a solution from above. The involvement of all stakeholders in the decision-making process helps build ownership and commitment to the solution.

Following the implementation of a solution, ongoing monitoring and evaluation are vital. Regular check-ins and feedback sessions should be held to assess the effectiveness of the solution and to identify any unforeseen consequences. If the solution is not working as intended, the team should be prepared to revise the approach or develop an alternative solution. This iterative process of refinement and adaptation ensures that the solution remains effective even as circumstances change.

Let's consider a real-world example: A marketing team launching a new product experienced a conflict over the marketing campaign's strategy. The creative team favored a bold unconventional approach, while the sales team preferred a more traditional, data-driven strategy. This conflict, initially characterized by heated debates and personal accusations, was addressed through a series of facilitated workshops. These workshops focused on identifying the underlying concerns of each team: the creative team valued innovation and brand impact, while the sales team prioritized measurable results and return on investment. Through open discussions, each team understood the other's perspective, allowing for a collaborative brainstorming session. The result was a hybrid strategy, incorporating elements of both approaches to strike a balance between creativity and data-driven decision-making. This process not only resolved the conflict but also fostered a stronger collaborative relationship between the creative and sales teams, enhancing future projects.

In another case, a software development team faced conflict over resource allocation. One team was facing a tight deadline, while another had excess capacity. The initial response was to simply allocate more resources to the pressured team, but this approach proved insufficient. Further investigation revealed the root cause: a lack of clear communication and coordination between the teams. The project manager, acting as a facilitator, helped identify areas where tasks could be reassigned, leveraging the excess capacity in the other team. The teams were encouraged to collaborate directly, using project management tools for transparent task tracking. This fostered better communication and coordination, resulting in improved collaboration and conflict resolution. The team not only met its deadlines but also learned valuable lessons in effective resource management and inter-team communication.

These examples underscore the importance of a proactive, systematic approach to conflict management in adaptive teams. By fostering open communication, identifying root causes, facilitating constructive discussions, and implementing mutually acceptable solutions, adaptive teams can transform conflict from a potential obstacle into a catalyst for growth and innovation. It's not merely about resolving disagreements; it's about strengthening relationships, building trust, and creating a more resilient and productive team. The ability to manage conflict effectively is a critical competency for any adaptive team navigating the complexities of today's dynamic environment. The investment in conflict management skills ultimately pays dividends in improved team performance, innovation, and overall success.

Measuring and Improving Team Performance

Measuring and improving team performance within the dynamic context of an adaptive organization requires a shift from traditional, static metrics to those that reflect the inherent fluidity and responsiveness of the team. Simply tracking output or meeting deadlines, while important, fails to capture the essence of adaptive capability. Instead, we need to focus on metrics that reveal the team's ability to learn, adapt, and improve continuously in the face of uncertainty.

One crucial KPI for adaptive teams is the speed of response . The ability to react swiftly and effectively to changing circumstances is paramount. This doesn't simply mean speed in completing tasks; it encompasses the entire process from identifying a challenge, analyzing its implications, developing a response, and implementing it. Tracking the time elapsed between recognizing a problem and implementing a solution provides a valuable measure of the team's responsiveness. This requires establishing clear processes for issue identification, escalation, and resolution, coupled with a robust communication system to ensure that information flows efficiently. Analyzing the speed of response across different types of challenges – some predictable, others completely novel – helps reveal potential bottlenecks and areas for improvement. For instance, a team consistently slow to adapt to unexpected market shifts indicates a need for enhanced forecasting capabilities or a more flexible operational structure.

Another essential metric is problem-solving effectiveness. Adaptive teams are inherently problem-solving machines, continuously navigating challenges and finding innovative solutions. Measuring this effectiveness requires going beyond simply counting the number of problems solved. It involves evaluating the quality of solutions, their long-term impact, and the team's ability to learn from past experiences. This can involve tracking factors such as the originality of solutions, their efficiency, their cost-effectiveness, and their sustainability. Post-project reviews, facilitated discussions, and the use of retrospective tools can be valuable in assessing the team's problem-solving capabilities and identifying areas needing improvement. Consider, for instance, a team that consistently develops elegant and scalable solutions to complex problems, versus another team that finds temporary fixes that become unsustainable in the long run. The difference lies in their problem-solving approach, which can be measured and improved through training and better processes.

Team morale and engagement are also crucial indicators of adaptive team performance. High morale fosters a culture of collaboration, innovation, and willingness to embrace change, all essential ingredients for successful adaptation. Regular surveys, feedback sessions, and one-on-one conversations with team members can provide insights into morale levels, and identify any underlying issues impacting the team's performance. Tracking metrics like employee satisfaction, absenteeism rates, and turnover rates provide valuable quantitative data that can be correlated with specific team activities or challenges. Moreover, qualitatively assessing the team's collaborative dynamics through observation and team reflection activities can offer a deeper understanding of the factors driving morale. A team with high morale is more likely to be proactive, resilient, and adaptable to changing circumstances. A drop in morale, however, may indicate underlying issues that need attention, such as excessive workload, lack of recognition, or poor communication.

Beyond these core metrics, adaptive teams might also track other KPIs relevant to their specific context and industry. For example, a product development team might track the frequency of successful product launches, customer satisfaction ratings, and the speed of adapting to customer feedback. A marketing team might track campaign performance metrics, brand awareness scores, and the effectiveness of responses to market fluctuations. These specific KPIs offer insights into the effectiveness of adaptive strategies within the team's unique operating environment.

Improving team performance requires a multifaceted approach involving consistent monitoring, regular feedback, and iterative adjustments. Tracking the above-mentioned metrics is only the first step. The next crucial step is translating these data into actionable insights. This requires analyzing trends, identifying areas for improvement, and implementing targeted interventions. Regular feedback sessions, conducted both formally and informally, are essential. Team members should be encouraged to share their experiences, provide constructive criticism, and suggest improvements to the team's processes and methodologies.

Implementing effective feedback mechanisms requires a culture of open communication and psychological safety. Team members should feel comfortable expressing concerns, offering alternative perspectives, and admitting mistakes without fear of reprisal. The leader's role in fostering such an environment is paramount. Constructive feedback should be delivered in a timely, specific, and actionable manner. It's not enough to simply point out shortcomings; the feedback should also include suggestions for improvement and create an opportunity for open discussion and collaborative problem-solving.

Furthermore, adapting team structures and processes based on performance data is crucial. If a particular approach proves ineffective, the team should be willing to experiment with alternative methods. This might involve adjusting roles and responsibilities, streamlining workflows, or adopting new technologies. The key is to maintain a culture of continuous improvement, constantly learning and adapting based on experience and data. Agile methodologies, with their emphasis on iterative development and feedback loops, can be particularly useful in adaptive settings. Regular sprint retrospectives, for example, provide structured opportunities for reflection and improvement.

Let's consider a real-world example. A software development team facing frequent project delays implemented a system for tracking their speed of response to bugs and issues. By monitoring the time elapsed between bug identification and resolution, they identified a bottleneck in the testing phase. This led to a restructuring of the testing team, with additional resources allocated to the most critical areas. This intervention, driven by data, reduced project delays significantly, improving both speed and quality.

Simultaneously, they implemented regular feedback sessions to improve team morale and address communication issues, which had also contributed to the previous delays. The combination of data-driven interventions and a focus on improving team processes demonstrated a holistic approach to adaptive team performance improvement.

In another scenario, a marketing team struggling to adapt to changing market trends began tracking their problem-solving effectiveness using a scoring system based on the originality and impact of their campaign adjustments. Low scores highlighted a lack of creative thinking and insufficient market research. Subsequently, the team underwent training in creative problem-solving and enhanced their market research methods. This resulted in a noticeable improvement in their ability to adapt to market changes and generate effective campaigns. They incorporated regular reviews and feedback sessions to analyze the effectiveness of the implemented changes.

These examples emphasize that measuring and improving adaptive team performance is not a one-time event but an ongoing process. It requires a commitment to continuous learning, data-driven decision-making, and a culture that values open communication, collaboration, and adaptation. By implementing a robust system for tracking key performance indicators, providing timely and constructive feedback, and adapting team structures and processes as needed, organizations can cultivate high-performing adaptive teams capable of thriving in today's dynamic and unpredictable environment. The investment in these processes ultimately translates into enhanced organizational agility, innovation, and overall success.

Chapter 7: Utilizing Technology for Adaptive Leadership

Leveraging Data and Analytics for Informed Decision Making

Building upon the foundation of adaptive team performance, we now dive into the critical role of data and analytics in empowering adaptive leadership. Relying solely on intuition or gut feeling is a recipe for stagnation. Effective adaptive leadership hinges on the ability to anticipate change,
interpret complex patterns, and make informed decisions based on robust evidence. This requires a profound shift towards data-driven decision-making, leveraging the power of business intelligence to navigate uncertainty and capitalize on emerging opportunities.

The first step in harnessing the power of data is recognizing its inherent potential. Data, in its raw form, is merely a collection of facts and figures. It becomes powerful when transformed into actionable insights through rigorous analysis and interpretation. This necessitates a proactive approach to data collection, ensuring that relevant information is captured and stored systematically. This may involve implementing new data capture systems, integrating disparate data sources, or refining existing data collection processes. The key is to ensure comprehensive data coverage, minimizing gaps and biases that can skew analysis and lead to flawed conclusions.

Once the data is collected, the next crucial step involves the selection of appropriate analytical tools and techniques. The choice of tools depends on the nature of the data, the specific questions being asked, and the desired level of detail in the analysis. Simple descriptive statistics can provide a quick overview of key trends and patterns, while more sophisticated techniques like regression analysis, predictive modeling, and machine learning algorithms can reveal more nuanced relationships and predict future outcomes. The use of business intelligence dashboards allows for the real-time monitoring of key performance indicators (KPIs) and provides a visual representation of data trends, enabling leaders to quickly assess the organization's performance and identify potential risks or opportunities. Tools facilitating A/B testing provide a valuable way to compare different approaches and refine strategies based on quantitative results, optimizing for efficiency and maximizing impact.

However, the value of data analysis goes beyond merely identifying trends and patterns. It is equally crucial to interpret the data within its broader context. This involves considering external factors such as market conditions, technological advancements, and geopolitical events. A decline in sales, for example, might be attributed to a general economic downturn rather than an inherent problem with the product or service. Therefore, effective data interpretation necessitates a holistic approach, integrating quantitative data with qualitative insights gathered through surveys, customer feedback, and market research. This allows for a more comprehensive understanding of the situation, enabling the leader to form a more nuanced and accurate perspective.

Data visualization plays a critical role in facilitating effective communication and decision-making. Presenting complex data in a clear and concise manner is crucial, enabling stakeholders to grasp key insights quickly and easily. This requires a strong understanding of data visualization principles and the ability to choose the most appropriate chart or graph for the specific data being presented. Simple yet effective tools such as bar charts, line graphs, and pie charts can highlight key trends and comparisons, while more advanced visualization techniques can reveal complex relationships and patterns. Interactive dashboards, capable of presenting data in multiple ways and drilling down into granular detail, enhance understanding and empower stakeholders to engage actively in decision-making. The ability to effectively visualize data, transforming raw numbers into compelling stories, is a vital skill for adaptive leaders.

Let's consider some practical examples of how data analytics can support adaptive leadership. A retail company facing declining sales might use customer purchase data to identify changing consumer preferences. By analyzing purchasing patterns, the company can discern emerging trends, anticipate future demand, and adjust its product offerings accordingly. This proactive approach allows the company to adapt to market changes before they significantly impact its profitability. Analyzing website traffic data, social media interactions, and customer service interactions provides a comprehensive picture of customer sentiment, allowing the company to identify areas for improvement in its products, services, and overall customer experience. This data-driven approach to customer understanding enables the company to make targeted improvements and enhance its brand loyalty.

In the manufacturing sector, predictive maintenance leverages sensor data from machinery to predict equipment failures before they occur. This allows for proactive maintenance scheduling, minimizing downtime, optimizing production efficiency, and reducing maintenance costs. By anticipating potential disruptions and proactively addressing them, the organization can maintain its operational efficiency and enhance its overall resilience. The use of real-time data monitoring enables immediate identification of production bottlenecks, facilitating rapid response and adjustments to operational processes, leading to continuous improvement in efficiency and output.

In the healthcare industry, data analytics can enhance patient care. Analyzing patient records and health metrics can help identify high-risk patients, allowing healthcare providers to intervene proactively and improve health outcomes. This data-driven approach to risk management empowers healthcare professionals to personalize treatment plans and enhance the overall quality of care. The analysis of epidemiological data can assist in identifying disease outbreaks and informing public health interventions, enabling proactive measures to contain the spread of infectious diseases.

These examples highlight the transformative power of data analytics in supporting adaptive leadership across various sectors. It allows leaders to make informed decisions, anticipate change, and effectively navigate the uncertainties of the modern business environment. However, effective utilization of data requires more than just the technical expertise to analyze data; it also necessitates a cultural shift within the organization. A data-driven culture fosters an environment where data is valued, shared, and actively used to inform decision-making at all levels. This requires leadership buy-in, training and development programs for employees, and the establishment of clear processes for data collection, analysis, and interpretation. The investment in creating a data-driven culture ultimately pays off through enhanced organizational agility, improved decision-making, and increased organizational resilience.

Ethical considerations are paramount in the use of data analytics. Data privacy and security must be prioritized, ensuring that data is collected, used, and stored in a responsible and ethical manner. Transparency and accountability are vital in maintaining trust with stakeholders. Leaders must ensure that data is used fairly and equitably, avoiding biases that could lead to discriminatory outcomes. By adhering to ethical principles, organizations can build trust with their customers, employees, and other stakeholders, fostering a positive and sustainable relationship with the data they utilize. A clear ethical framework guiding data collection, analysis, and use is essential to maintain integrity and build long-term trust.

Leveraging data and analytics for informed decision-making is not merely a technological enhancement; it's a fundamental shift in leadership philosophy. It empowers leaders to move beyond reactive management to proactive anticipation, fostering a culture of continuous learning and improvement. By embracing data-driven decision-making, organizations can cultivate greater agility, enhance resilience, and achieve sustainable success in the face of ever-changing circumstances. The integration of data analytics into leadership strategies is no longer an option; it is a necessity for business survival. The journey towards becoming a truly data-driven organization requires a commitment to continuous learning, adaptation, and a dedication to ethical principles that will safeguard the trust and integrity of the organization.

Utilizing Collaboration and Communication Technologies

Building on the critical role of data-driven decision-making in adaptive leadership, we now turn our attention to the equally crucial aspect of leveraging technology to enhance collaboration and communication. In today's interconnected world, effective communication and seamless information sharing are no longer luxuries but necessities for organizational success. This is particularly true in environments characterized by rapid change and uncertainty, where the ability to adapt quickly and respond effectively to emerging challenges is paramount. The appropriate utilization of technology can significantly amplify the effectiveness of adaptive leadership by fostering collaboration, accelerating decision-making, and improving organizational responsiveness.

The range of technological tools available for enhancing collaboration and communication is vast and diverse, spanning from simple email and instant messaging applications to sophisticated project management software and advanced video conferencing platforms. The optimal selection of tools depends on the specific needs and context of the organization, taking into consideration factors such as the size of the team, the nature of the work being undertaken, and the geographical distribution of team members. A carefully considered technology strategy is paramount to maximizing the benefits of these tools, avoiding the pitfalls of technology overload, and ensuring their effective integration into the organizational workflow.

Project management software, for instance, provides a centralized platform for managing tasks, deadlines, and resources. Tools like Asana, Trello, and Monday.com offer features such as task assignment, progress tracking, and collaborative document editing. These tools not only streamline workflow and improve organizational efficiency but also enhance transparency and accountability, enabling team members to monitor progress, identify potential bottlenecks, and proactively address challenges. The centralized nature of these platforms minimizes the risk of information silos, ensuring that all team members have access to the most up-to-date information and can contribute effectively to the collective effort. Furthermore, many project management platforms incorporate features that enable communication, such as integrated chat functions and discussion forums, promoting real-time feedback and seamless collaboration.

Beyond project management, video conferencing platforms play a crucial role in fostering effective communication, particularly in geographically dispersed teams. Zoom, Microsoft Teams, and Google Meet have become indispensable tools for conducting virtual meetings, workshops, and training sessions. These platforms allow for real-time interaction, enabling participants to engage in meaningful discussions, share ideas, and build relationships. The ability to see and hear each other enhances communication effectiveness, fostering a sense of connection and facilitating a more engaging and collaborative experience. These tools often incorporate features such as screen sharing and collaborative document editing, allowing teams to work on projects simultaneously and share information seamlessly. The use of video conferencing is not limited to formal meetings; it can be used for informal check-ins, fostering a sense of community and strengthening team cohesion.

Instant messaging applications, such as Slack, Microsoft Teams, and Google Chat, are invaluable for facilitating quick and easy communication. They allow team members to exchange information instantaneously, ask quick questions, and share updates without the formality of email or scheduled meetings. This fosters a more agile and responsive communication style, allowing teams to respond quickly to changing circumstances and adapt to unexpected challenges. The use of designated channels for specific projects or topics ensures that information remains organized and easily accessible, minimizing information overload and maximizing efficiency. These platforms often integrate with other collaboration tools, such as project management software and video conferencing platforms, creating a seamless ecosystem for communication and collaboration.

However, simply adopting these technologies isn't enough to guarantee improved collaboration and communication. Effective utilization requires a well-defined strategy, appropriate training for employees, and a commitment to fostering a culture that embraces technology as a means to enhance communication and teamwork. This includes establishing clear guidelines for communication protocols, defining roles and responsibilities for managing communication channels, and providing ongoing support and training to ensure employees are comfortable using the chosen technologies effectively. Failure to address these aspects can lead to technology becoming a barrier rather than a facilitator of effective communication.

For instance, the widespread adoption of email, while seemingly straightforward, can quickly lead to information overload and decreased efficiency if not managed properly. An effective email strategy includes guidelines for subject lines, email length, response times, and the use of email distribution lists. This ensures that information is conveyed clearly and efficiently, avoiding the clutter that can hinder communication. Similarly, the use of instant messaging tools requires clear protocols for communication etiquette and the appropriate use of channels to avoid disrupting workflows.

The effective use of technology for collaboration and communication requires addressing the potential challenges associated with remote work. Maintaining a strong sense of community and fostering team cohesion when team members are geographically dispersed requires proactive effort. Regular virtual team-building activities, social interactions, and opportunities for informal communication can help to mitigate the sense of isolation that can occur in remote work environments. Clear communication protocols and the consistent use of chosen technologies help maintain transparency and ensure that everyone is kept informed, minimizing misunderstandings and maximizing collaboration.

The integration of collaboration and communication technologies into the organizational culture requires leadership buy-in and commitment. Leaders need to demonstrate a clear understanding of the benefits of these technologies and actively champion their adoption. Providing ongoing support, training, and resources is crucial to ensuring that employees are comfortable using the chosen technologies effectively and are empowered to utilize them to enhance their work. This might involve offering workshops, providing access to online resources, and embedding technology integration into existing professional development initiatives.

The effective utilization of collaboration and communication technologies is a crucial component of adaptive leadership. By embracing the appropriate tools and implementing a well-defined strategy, organizations can foster a culture of seamless information sharing, enhance teamwork, and accelerate decision-making. This requires not only the adoption of the right technology but also a commitment to fostering a culture that values collaboration, embraces innovation, and empowers employees to utilize technology effectively to enhance their work and contribute to the organization's overall success. The seamless integration of these technologies, combined with a strong leadership commitment, creates a synergistic effect, allowing organizations to adapt more quickly to change, respond to challenges more effectively, and ultimately achieve greater success. The proactive implementation and skillful application of these tools are not merely technological advancements, but fundamental shifts in how work is performed and how teams interact – a crucial element of the adaptive leadership strategy.

Employing AI and Machine Learning for Predictive Analysis

Building upon the previous discussion of technology's role in enhancing collaboration and communication, we now look into a particularly powerful application: the use of artificial intelligence (AI) and machine learning (ML) for predictive analysis in adaptive leadership. Predictive analysis, powered by AI and ML, represents a significant leap forward in organizational foresight, enabling leaders to anticipate future trends and challenges with greater accuracy than ever before. This allows for proactive adaptation and strategic pivoting, a cornerstone of effective adaptive leadership.

The core function of AI and ML in this context is to analyze vast quantities of data – historical performance metrics, market trends, customer behavior, competitor activities, and even social media sentiment – to identify patterns and predict future outcomes. This surpasses the capabilities of human analysis alone, which is often limited by cognitive biases, information overload, and the inherent limitations of processing vast datasets. AI algorithms, however, can sift through this data with unprecedented speed and accuracy, identifying subtle correlations and trends that might otherwise remain unnoticed.

For instance, consider a retail company facing fluctuating demand. Traditional forecasting methods might rely on historical sales data and expert judgment, but AI can integrate a far broader range of data sources: weather patterns affecting customer traffic, social media buzz about competing products, real-time inventory levels, and even economic indicators. By processing this multi-faceted data, the AI model can generate significantly more accurate demand forecasts, allowing the company to optimize inventory management, staffing levels, and marketing campaigns proactively. This prevents overstocking or stockouts, minimizes waste, and maximizes profitability – all critical aspects of adaptive leadership in a volatile market.

Similarly, in the healthcare industry, AI-powered predictive analysis can be used to anticipate outbreaks of infectious diseases. By analyzing data from various sources – patient records, geographical information systems, and public health reports – the AI can identify early warning signs and predict potential hotspots, enabling public health officials to deploy resources and interventions proactively, minimizing the impact of outbreaks. This is a prime example of adaptive leadership in action, utilizing technology to respond quickly and effectively to emerging threats.

In the financial sector, AI and ML are utilized to detect and prevent fraud. By analyzing transaction data, identifying patterns indicative of fraudulent activity, and flagging suspicious transactions for human review, these technologies significantly reduce financial losses and maintain the integrity of financial systems. The proactive identification and prevention of fraud showcase the crucial role of predictive analysis in maintaining stability and adapting to evolving threats in dynamic environments.

The application of AI in predictive analysis extends far beyond these examples. In manufacturing, AI can predict equipment failures, minimizing downtime and optimizing maintenance schedules. In human resources, AI can analyze employee data to predict attrition rates, enabling proactive interventions to improve employee retention. In supply chain management, AI can predict disruptions, allowing companies to mitigate risks and maintain operational efficiency. The versatility of AI and ML makes them invaluable tools across numerous industries, enabling proactive adaptation and improved decision-making.

However, the implementation of AI and ML for predictive analysis is not without its challenges. One critical aspect is data quality. AI algorithms are only as good as the data they are trained on. Inaccurate, incomplete, or biased data will lead to inaccurate predictions. Therefore, meticulous data cleaning, validation, and preprocessing are crucial steps in ensuring the reliability and accuracy of AI-driven predictions.

Another challenge is the interpretability of AI models. Many advanced AI algorithms, particularly deep learning models, are "black boxes," meaning that their decision-making
processes are not easily understood by humans. This lack of transparency can be a significant concern, particularly in high-stakes situations where understanding the rationale behind a prediction is essential. Therefore, it's crucial to select and implement AI models that offer a degree of interpretability, allowing leaders to understand the factors

driving the predictions and make informed decisions based on a clear understanding of the underlying logic.

Ethical considerations are also paramount. AI algorithms can perpetuate and amplify existing biases present in the data they are trained on, leading to unfair or discriminatory outcomes. For example, an AI system used for hiring decisions might inadvertently discriminate against certain demographic groups if the training data reflects historical biases in hiring practices. Therefore, careful attention must be paid to data fairness and algorithmic transparency to ensure ethical and responsible use of AI in leadership and management. Regular audits and evaluations of AI systems are essential to detect and mitigate potential biases.

The responsible use of AI requires a clear understanding of its limitations. AI is a tool, not a replacement for human judgment. While AI can provide valuable insights and predictions, it should be used to augment, not replace, human decision-making. Leaders should view AI as a powerful partner in decision-making, providing valuable data and insights, but retaining ultimate responsibility for the decisions made.

To effectively integrate AI and ML into their leadership practices, organizations need to establish a robust data infrastructure, invest in the necessary technical expertise, and cultivate a data-driven culture. This requires providing training and development opportunities for employees to build their data literacy skills and understand how AI and ML can enhance their work. Additionally, establishing clear ethical guidelines and processes for the development and deployment of AI systems is crucial to ensuring responsible and ethical use.

Successful implementation of AI in predictive analysis requires a holistic approach. This includes not only the technical aspects of data collection, model development, and deployment, but also the human aspects of organizational culture, leadership buy-in, and ethical considerations. A commitment to continuous learning, adaptation, and a willingness to embrace change are essential to effectively leverage the transformative potential of AI for adaptive leadership.

The application of AI and machine learning for predictive analysis represents a powerful tool for enhancing adaptive leadership. By leveraging the capabilities of these technologies, organizations can anticipate future trends, identify potential risks, and make more informed decisions, enabling proactive adaptation and improved organizational performance. However, responsible and ethical implementation requires careful attention to data quality, algorithmic transparency, ethical considerations, and the crucial role of human judgment in the decision-making process. The successful integration of AI into the leadership toolkit requires a multifaceted strategy that embraces both technological advancement and human-centered leadership principles. The future of adaptive leadership lies in the harmonious synergy between human ingenuity and the analytical power of AI, creating a powerful force for organizational success in an increasingly complex and dynamic world.

Automating Processes for Increased Efficiency and Adaptability

Automating processes is no longer a futuristic concept; it's a critical element of adaptive leadership. The ability to streamline operations, enhance efficiency, and improve responsiveness to change is paramount for organizations aiming to thrive in a dynamic environment. Let's take a look into the practical application of automation, highlighting its transformative potential and addressing the necessary considerations for successful implementation.

The first step in automating processes involves a thorough assessment of current workflows. Identifying tasks that are repetitive, time-consuming, and prone to human error is crucial. These are prime candidates for automation. Consider, for instance, a customer service department inundated with routine inquiries about order status, shipping information, or return policies. Implementing a chatbot powered by natural language processing (NLP) can significantly reduce the burden on human agents, freeing them to handle more complex and nuanced customer issues. This not only enhances efficiency but also improves customer satisfaction by providing instant and accurate responses.

Similarly, in finance departments, automating tasks such as invoice processing, expense reports, and reconciliation can significantly reduce processing time, minimize errors, and free up valuable human resources for more strategic activities. Software solutions equipped with optical character recognition (OCR) can automatically extract data from invoices and other documents, eliminating manual data entry and reducing the risk of human error. Robotic process automation (RPA) can automate repetitive tasks such as data validation, report generation, and data migration, further enhancing efficiency and accuracy.

Moving beyond the back-office functions, we find significant opportunities for automation in manufacturing and supply chain management. In manufacturing, automated systems can manage inventory levels, optimize production schedules and monitor equipment performance, minimizing downtime and maximizing efficiency. Sensors integrated into machinery can detect anomalies and predict potential equipment failures, allowing for proactive maintenance and preventing costly production disruptions. This proactive approach to maintenance is a hallmark of adaptive leadership, preventing problems before they escalate and ensuring continuous operational flow.

In the supply chain, automation plays a pivotal role in enhancing agility and responsiveness to market fluctuations. Real-time tracking of goods using GPS and RFID technology provides better visibility into the supply chain, enabling companies to quickly respond to disruptions and optimize delivery routes. Automated warehouse systems, using robotics and automated guided vehicles (AGVs), can significantly improve the efficiency of picking, packing, and shipping processes, reducing lead times and improving customer satisfaction. Predictive analytics, as discussed in the previous section, can be integrated with these automated systems to forecast demand and optimize inventory levels, preventing stockouts and minimizing waste.

However, the successful implementation of automation requires careful consideration of its potential impact on the workforce. Automation can displace workers performing repetitive tasks, leading to job losses and potential employee anxieties. Addressing this concern requires a proactive and empathetic approach. Reskilling and upskilling initiatives should be implemented to equip employees with the skills needed to manage and operate automated systems. This transition should be viewed as an opportunity for workforce development, empowering employees with new capabilities and enabling them to take on more complex and higher-value roles.

A robust communication strategy is also essential to ensure transparency and manage expectations during the automation process. Employees should be involved in the planning and implementation phases, allowing them to voice their concerns and contribute their expertise. This participatory approach can foster buy-in and ensure a smoother transition, minimizing resistance and fostering collaboration.

Successful automation initiatives require a holistic approach, encompassing not only the technological aspects but also the organizational and human dimensions. Establishing clear goals and metrics, conducting thorough risk assessments, and developing a comprehensive change management plan are crucial for success. This includes selecting the right automation technologies, integrating them with existing systems, and providing comprehensive training and support to employees.

Several organizations have demonstrated the transformative potential of automation in achieving adaptive leadership. Companies like Amazon have invested heavily in automated warehousing and delivery systems, enhancing their efficiency and responsiveness to customer demand. Similarly, many manufacturing companies have implemented automated production lines, leading to increased output and improved product quality. These examples demonstrate the tangible benefits of automation when implemented strategically and with careful consideration of its impact on the workforce.

Ultimately, automation is not merely about replacing human labor with machines; it's about enhancing human capabilities and enabling greater efficiency, adaptability, and responsiveness. By strategically automating processes and investing in employee development, organizations can build more agile, resilient, and successful organizations, able to navigate the complexities of a rapidly changing world. The future of adaptive leadership is not about choosing between humans and machines, but about leveraging the unique strengths of both to create a truly synergistic and highly effective organization. This requires a continuous cycle of assessment, adaptation, and improvement, ensuring that automation remains a strategic enabler of adaptive leadership, rather than a static solution to a dynamic challenge. The journey towards a fully automated, responsive organization is not a destination, but an ongoing process requiring continuous monitoring and improvement, mirroring the very essence of adaptive leadership itself. The key is to view automation not as a threat, but as a catalyst for enhanced performance, workforce development, and sustained competitiveness. This requires a strategic vision that aligns technological advancements with human capital development, creating a symbiotic relationship between technology and talent. Only then can organizations truly unlock the transformative potential of automation and build a future where technology empowers, rather than replaces, human ingenuity and adaptability.

Integrating Technology and Human Intelligence for Optimal Outcomes

The preceding sections have explored the transformative potential of technology in fostering adaptive leadership, focusing on automation's role in streamlining operations and enhancing efficiency. However, the true power of technology in navigating a dynamic landscape lies not in replacing human intelligence but in augmenting it, creating a powerful synergy between human ingenuity and technological capabilities. This integration is crucial for achieving optimal outcomes and ensuring that technological advancements serve as enablers of adaptive leadership, rather than impediments.

The human element remains irreplaceable in the leadership equation. While technology can automate repetitive tasks and analyze vast datasets with incredible speed and accuracy, it lacks the critical thinking, creativity, and emotional intelligence essential for truly effective leadership. Human judgment is vital in interpreting data, making nuanced decisions, and adapting strategies based on evolving circumstances. Technology can provide insights and predictions, but it is the human leader who ultimately decides how to act upon that information. This requires a deep understanding of organizational context, ethical considerations, and the potential impact of decisions on individuals and the broader ecosystem.

Consider, for instance, the use of predictive analytics in supply chain management. Sophisticated algorithms can forecast demand and optimize inventory levels, minimizing waste and ensuring timely delivery. However, unforeseen events—a natural disaster, a geopolitical crisis, or a sudden shift in consumer preferences—can disrupt even the most accurate predictions. In such situations, human judgment and adaptability become paramount. The ability to interpret the unpredictable, assess risks, and make informed decisions in the face of uncertainty is a critical skill that technology cannot replicate. The human leader needs to leverage technological insights but also possess the flexibility and foresight to adjust strategies based on real-time information and evolving circumstances.

Technology's role extends beyond mere efficiency gains. It facilitates innovation and creativity by providing access to vast repositories of information and enabling the exploration of new possibilities. Tools such as machine learning and artificial intelligence can identify patterns and insights that may be overlooked by human analysts, sparking new ideas and approaches to problem-solving.

However, the translation of these insights into actionable strategies, the conceptualization of innovative solutions, and the articulation of a compelling vision for the future all require human creativity and strategic thinking. Human leaders play a crucial role in guiding the process of innovation, fostering a culture of experimentation, and ensuring that technological advancements are used to drive meaningful organizational change.

The effective integration of technology and human intelligence requires a deliberate and strategic approach. It's not merely about implementing new technologies; it's about cultivating a culture that embraces both human expertise and technological capabilities. This involves several key elements:

Investing in human capital:
Organizations must invest in training and development to equip their workforce with the skills needed to effectively utilize and manage new technologies. This includes not only technical skills but also critical thinking, problem-solving, and adaptability skills. A digitally literate workforce is crucial for harnessing the full potential of technological advancements.

Fostering collaboration:
Effective leadership requires fostering collaboration between humans and machines. This means creating systems and processes that enable seamless interaction between human decision-makers and technological tools. It's about designing workflows that leverage the strengths of both human intelligence and technological capabilities,

creating a synergistic relationship that drives optimal outcomes.

Promoting ethical considerations:
As organizations increasingly rely on technology, ethical considerations become paramount. Data privacy, algorithmic bias, and the potential impact of automation on the workforce must be addressed proactively. Human oversight and ethical guidelines are essential to ensure that technology is used responsibly and ethically, mitigating potential risks and ensuring alignment with organizational values.

Embracing continuous learning:
The rapid pace of technological advancement demands a culture of continuous learning and adaptation. Leaders must be committed to staying abreast of the latest technological trends and their implications for their organizations. This involves not only formal training but also informal learning opportunities, such as attending industry conferences, engaging with thought leaders, and fostering a culture of experimentation and continuous improvement.

Several leading companies exemplify the successful integration of technology and human intelligence in their leadership approaches. Consider companies like Google, which uses advanced AI algorithms to analyze massive datasets and identify trends, but relies heavily on human judgment to interpret these findings and make strategic decisions. Their success is not solely attributable to their technological prowess but also to their ability to effectively integrate human intelligence with technological capabilities.

Similarly, companies like Netflix leverage data analytics to understand consumer preferences and personalize content recommendations. However, their success also hinges on the creativity and judgment of their human teams in developing new content and crafting a compelling user experience. The interaction between data-driven insights and human creativity is at the heart of their adaptive leadership approach.

The effective use of technology in adaptive leadership is not simply about automating tasks. It's about creating a system where technology enhances human capabilities and fosters a culture of continuous learning and adaptation. It is about using technology to empower human decision-making, fostering innovation, and driving organizational agility. By embracing this symbiotic relationship, organizations can navigate the complexities of a rapidly changing world, achieving optimal outcomes and building resilient, forward-thinking organizations. The ultimate aim is not to replace human leadership with artificial intelligence, but to create a powerful, synergistic partnership that leverages the strengths of both, leading to a more agile, innovative, and successful future. This integrated approach, prioritizing ethical considerations and continuous learning, forms the cornerstone of future-proof leadership in a world increasingly shaped by technological advancements. This ongoing evolution requires a commitment to flexibility, a willingness to embrace change, and a deep understanding of the interplay between human potential and technological innovation. Only then can organizations truly realize the transformative power of technology in adaptive leadership, driving sustainable growth and long-term success.

Chapter 8: Case Studies in Adaptive Leadership

Case Study A Technology Company Navigating Disruption

The previous discussion highlighted the crucial interplay between human intelligence and technological capabilities in fostering adaptive leadership. We explored how technology can augment human decision-making, enhance efficiency, and drive innovation, but stressed the irreplaceable role of human judgment, creativity, and emotional intelligence. This symbiotic relationship, however, is not always straightforward. Navigating the complexities of technological disruption requires a deep understanding of organizational dynamics and a willingness to embrace significant change. The following case study illustrates these challenges and the strategies employed by a technology company to successfully adapt to a rapidly evolving market.

This case study centers on a mid-sized technology company, let's call it "InnovateTech," specializing in software solutions for the financial services sector. InnovateTech had enjoyed considerable success for over a decade, building a reputation for reliable, albeit somewhat conventional, software products. Their organizational structure was traditional, with clearly defined hierarchies and a strong emphasis on established processes. Leadership was largely top-down, with a focus on execution and meeting predetermined targets. While innovation was encouraged, it was channeled through well-defined R&D departments, following a methodical, incremental approach. The disruption arrived in the form of a new, cloud-based competitor, "CloudFin," offering a more agile, customizable, and cost-effective solution. CloudFin's platform leveraged advanced AI and machine learning capabilities, offering features far beyond InnovateTech's existing offerings.

Suddenly, InnovateTech's established market position faced a significant threat. Their clients, attracted by CloudFin's innovative technology and competitive pricing, began to consider switching platforms. InnovateTech's initial response was defensive. They focused on emphasizing their long-standing reputation and the perceived stability of their on-premise solutions. However, this strategy proved ineffective. The market was clearly shifting towards cloud-based solutions, and InnovateTech's traditional approach could not compete with CloudFin's disruptive technology.

The Leadership Pivot

The company's leadership, initially resistant to change, faced mounting pressure from both internal stakeholders (employees concerned about job security) and external stakeholders (clients seeking more modern solutions).

Recognizing the urgency of the situation, InnovateTech's CEO initiated a strategic review. This involved bringing together a diverse cross-functional team—including representatives from engineering, sales, marketing, and customer support—to analyze the competitive landscape and develop a comprehensive response. The team conducted a thorough assessment of CloudFin's capabilities, identifying their key strengths and weaknesses. Crucially, the review also included a candid assessment of InnovateTech's own internal weaknesses, acknowledging the limitations of their traditional organizational structure and decision-making processes.

A significant shift in leadership style was required. The CEO, recognizing the need for greater agility and responsiveness, began delegating more authority and empowering lower-level managers to make decisions. This decentralized approach fostered greater innovation and faster response times. In addition, the company invested heavily in employee training, providing opportunities for upskilling and reskilling in areas such as cloud computing, AI, and machine learning. This proactive approach aimed to equip InnovateTech's workforce with the skills necessary to compete in the changing market.

The company also made significant changes to its organizational structure. They adopted a more agile methodology, moving away from traditional waterfall processes to iterative development cycles. This enabled faster adaptation to market feedback and allowed for continuous improvement of their software offerings. A new product development team was established, specifically tasked with developing a cloud-based solution to compete with CloudFin. This team was given significant autonomy and empowered to experiment with new technologies and approaches, challenging the company's historical aversion to risk.

The development of InnovateTech's cloud-based platform involved significant challenges. The company faced internal resistance from employees accustomed to the traditional approach, and navigating the complexities of cloud technology proved demanding. However, the renewed leadership focus on collaboration, transparency, and empowerment significantly lessened resistance and fostered a more collaborative environment. Regular updates, open forums, and transparent communication about the company's progress played a vital role in maintaining employee morale and trust.

Over the next two years, InnovateTech successfully launched its cloud-based platform. The platform incorporated many of the features of CloudFin but with a greater emphasis on security and data privacy, addressing a critical customer concern. The marketing campaign focused on highlighting these strengths, emphasizing InnovateTech's reputation for reliability and customer support. The combination of a robust platform, effective marketing, and strong customer relationships allowed InnovateTech to regain market share.

This case study demonstrates several key principles of adaptive leadership in the face of technological disruption. First, it highlights the importance of honest self-assessment, acknowledging weaknesses and limitations, as a prerequisite for successful change. Second, it underscores the critical role of empowering employees and fostering a culture of collaboration and innovation. Third, it showcases the necessity of adopting agile methodologies to enable quick adaptation to market changes. Finally, it emphasizes the significance of continuous learning and development in navigating the complexities of technological advancement.

InnovateTech's success was not merely a matter of technological innovation but also a testament to the power of adaptive leadership in transforming organizational culture and strategy to meet the challenges of a rapidly evolving market.

The successful transition of InnovateTech highlights several critical factors beyond the technological implementation. The company's commitment to open communication and transparent leadership proved vital in mitigating employee anxiety and fostering a sense of shared purpose during the challenging transformation. Regular updates, town hall meetings, and open dialogue channels enabled the leadership to address concerns promptly, build trust, and ensure everyone felt involved in the company's strategic shift.

Moreover, InnovateTech's investment in employee training was not just a cost, but a strategic investment in human capital. The training programs were tailored to the specific needs of the company's technological transformation, equipping employees with the necessary skills to contribute effectively to the new cloud-based platform. This commitment showcased the leadership's recognition of employee value and their crucial role in the company's future success, leading to improved morale and increased employee retention.

Finally, InnovateTech's decision to focus on data privacy and security as a key differentiator demonstrated a keen understanding of the market and customer needs. While CloudFin's initial success was based on innovative features, InnovateTech capitalized on existing customer concerns around data security by highlighting their expertise and experience in this critical area. This strategic choice allowed them to offer a compelling alternative, effectively leveraging their existing strengths to compete in the new market landscape. The case of InnovateTech serves as a valuable lesson in the multifaceted nature of adaptive leadership, illustrating that successful adaptation requires not only technological innovation but also organizational restructuring, effective communication, and strategic prioritization of customer needs. It is a testament to the power of a holistic approach that integrates technological advancements with a deep understanding of human dynamics and organizational culture. The ultimate success hinges on the ability of the leadership to embrace change, empower their workforce, and cultivate a culture of continuous learning and adaptability, thereby ensuring that the organization remains resilient and responsive to the ever-shifting landscape of the technological world.

Case Study A Manufacturing Company Adapting to New Regulations

This case study focuses on "Precision Manufacturing," a medium-sized company specializing in the production of precision components for the aerospace industry. For decades, Precision Manufacturing had operated under a relatively stable regulatory environment, with well-established environmental guidelines. Their processes, while efficient, were not designed for the stringent requirements of the new, more environmentally conscious regulations. These new regulations, aimed at reducing carbon emissions and hazardous waste, presented a significant challenge to Precision Manufacturing's established operational model.

The initial response from Precision Manufacturing's leadership was characterized by a degree of apprehension and resistance to change. The company's leadership team, composed largely of individuals with extensive experience within the traditional manufacturing sector, initially viewed the new regulations as an unwelcome burden, adding complexity and cost to their operations. They focused on the immediate challenges of compliance, prioritizing short-term solutions over a more holistic, long-term strategic adaptation. This initial reactive approach, however, proved to be insufficient to address the complexities of the new regulatory environment.

The company's existing environmental management system (EMS) was inadequate to meet the heightened standards. Their previous practices, focused on meeting minimum compliance requirements, lacked the comprehensive approach needed to address the broader environmental impact of their operations. The initial attempts at compliance focused on piecemeal solutions, addressing individual requirements in isolation, rather than integrating them into a cohesive, company-wide strategy. This fragmented approach led to inefficiencies, increased costs, and ultimately, a lack of substantial progress towards full compliance.

Recognizing the limitations of their initial approach, Precision Manufacturing's CEO initiated a significant organizational shift. He assembled a cross-functional team, bringing together representatives from engineering, operations, environmental compliance, and legal departments. This team was tasked with conducting a thorough assessment of the new regulations and developing a comprehensive compliance strategy. This strategy involved not just meeting the minimum requirements but also identifying opportunities to enhance their environmental performance beyond mere compliance.

A critical element of this strategy was a shift in leadership style. The CEO moved away from a top-down, directive management approach and instead fostered a more collaborative and participative leadership style. He empowered team members to take ownership of specific aspects of the compliance initiative, encouraging them to contribute their expertise and ideas. This decentralized approach unleashed a surge of creative solutions and accelerated the implementation process.

One of the most impactful changes was the implementation of a robust, company-wide sustainability program. This program wasn't merely a checklist of regulatory requirements but rather a comprehensive initiative aimed at embedding sustainable practices into every aspect of the company's operations. This involved a significant investment in new technologies and processes designed to reduce energy consumption, minimize waste generation, and improve the overall environmental footprint of the company.

The implementation involved significant technological upgrades. The company invested in advanced manufacturing equipment, incorporating energy-efficient designs and improved waste management capabilities. They also implemented a sophisticated tracking system to monitor energy consumption, emissions, and waste generation, providing real-time data to inform decisions and track progress toward their sustainability goals. This level of technological advancement was pivotal in ensuring compliance but also offered significant operational efficiencies, leading to cost savings in the long term.

Alongside these technological advancements, Precision Manufacturing also invested heavily in employee training and development. The company implemented comprehensive training programs designed to educate employees about the new regulations, the importance of environmental sustainability, and the company's commitment to responsible environmental stewardship. The training program fostered a culture of environmental awareness, encouraging employees to actively participate in the compliance initiative and contribute their own ideas for improvement.

The company also recognized the importance of transparent communication throughout the entire process. Regular updates were provided to all employees, keeping them informed of the progress made, the challenges encountered, and the overall strategy for achieving compliance. This open communication strategy was vital in building trust and fostering a shared sense of purpose, encouraging employees' participation and mitigating potential resistance to change. This proactive communication also helped to manage expectations and prevent the spread of misinformation, which could have undermined morale and slowed down the implementation process.

Precision Manufacturing also engaged in extensive communication with external stakeholders, including government agencies, suppliers, and customers. This transparent approach helped build strong relationships with key stakeholders, fostering a collaborative environment that supported the company's compliance efforts. Regular meetings with regulatory bodies helped to build a collaborative relationship and address any questions or concerns promptly. Transparency also enhanced the company's reputation, reinforcing its commitment to sustainability an strengthening its relationship with customers.

The outcome of this comprehensive approach was a successful and timely transition to full compliance with the new regulations. Precision Manufacturing not only met the regulatory requirements but also exceeded expectations, achieving significant improvements in their environmental performance. The company's commitment to sustainability extended beyond mere compliance, becoming a core aspect of its corporate identity and a key differentiator in the marketplace. The new processes and technologies resulted in increased operational efficiency and cost savings, improving the company's bottom line while simultaneously enhancing its environmental performance.

The case study of Precision Manufacturing provides a compelling example of how adaptive leadership can effectively navigate significant regulatory changes. It highlights the importance of a holistic approach, integrating technological advancements, employee training, and open communication to drive successful implementation and achieve lasting positive impact. The company's transition showcases that compliance with stringent environmental regulations isn't just a cost but rather an opportunity to enhance efficiency, boost reputation, and ultimately strengthen the organization's long-term sustainability and competitive advantage. The integration of environmental considerations into the company's core business strategy has not only ensured compliance but has also elevated Precision Manufacturing's position as a responsible and forward-thinking leader within its industry. This adaptive approach demonstrates the potential for organizations to transform challenges into opportunities for growth and improved performance. The successful navigation of the regulatory changes by Precision Manufacturing reinforces the critical role of proactive leadership, strategic planning, and a company-wide commitment to sustainability in overcoming significant organizational challenges and seizing the associated opportunities. This showcases that compliance isn't a burden but a catalyst for innovation and enhanced operational efficiency.

Case Study A Nonprofit Organization Responding to a Crisis

This case study focuses on "Community Support Network" (CSN), a large non-profit organization providing essential services to vulnerable populations in a major metropolitan area. For over three decades, CSN had built a strong reputation for its reliable and effective programs, including food banks, homeless shelters, and job training initiatives. Their operational model, however, relied heavily on consistent government funding and a network of established partnerships with local businesses and volunteers. The arrival of a sudden and severe economic downturn, coupled with a significant reduction in government grants, presented CSN with an unprecedented crisis.

The initial response from CSN's leadership team, comprised primarily of experienced social workers and administrators, was characterized by a sense of shock and disorientation. The organization's long-term strategic plan, predicated on a stable funding stream, was rendered obsolete almost overnight. Their initial reactions prioritized immediate cost-cutting measures, focusing on reducing staff and curtailing services to maintain operational solvency. This reactive approach, while understandable given the urgency of the situation, proved to be unsustainable in the long term. The reductions in services caused a significant outcry from the community, impacting the very people CSN was established to support. Simultaneously, the reduction in staffing led to demoralization among the remaining employees, impacting overall productivity and efficiency.

The rapid decline in available resources forced the organization to confront a stark reality: their traditional operational model was fundamentally flawed. Their dependence on government funding and established partnerships, while providing stability in the past, left them highly vulnerable to external economic shocks. The initial crisis management strategy, focused solely on cost-cutting, failed to address the underlying systemic issues that exacerbated the organization's predicament. This narrow focus neglected the essential need for diversification of funding streams, the cultivation of new partnerships, and the development of more resilient operational structures.

Recognizing the limitations of their reactive approach, CSN's Executive Director, a seasoned non-profit leader, initiated a significant shift in the organization's leadership style. She moved away from a centralized, top-down management model and adopted a more collaborative and distributed leadership approach. This involved empowering mid-level managers and frontline staff to participate actively in the development and implementation of crisis response strategies. Regular brainstorming sessions, open forums, and collaborative workshops were introduced, fostering a culture of shared responsibility and collective problem-solving. This new approach recognized the invaluable insights and expertise possessed by individuals across the organization, who had firsthand experience of the challenges faced by the community they served.

A pivotal moment came during one of these collaborative workshops. A young social worker suggested exploring the potential of crowdfunding and online fundraising platforms to diversify CSN's funding sources. This idea, initially met with some skepticism given the organization's traditional fundraising methods, eventually gained traction through collaborative development and refinement. The team developed a compelling fundraising campaign highlighting the organization's ongoing commitment to community service, emphasizing the direct impact their programs had on individuals' lives. The campaign resonated deeply with the local community, attracting significant donations and showcasing the power of collective effort in responding to a crisis.

In parallel with the fundraising efforts, CSN initiated a comprehensive review of its operational efficiency. This involved analyzing each program's effectiveness, identifying areas of potential cost reduction without compromising quality of service, and exploring opportunities for streamlining administrative processes. This efficiency drive resulted in the implementation of new technologies, such as online scheduling systems and virtual communication platforms, that minimized administrative overhead while enhancing overall operational efficiency. This allowed for significant cost savings while improving the organization's reach and effectiveness. The adoption of these technologies also helped to reduce the carbon footprint of the organization's operations, enhancing its overall sustainability.

CSN also placed a strong emphasis on cultivating new partnerships with the local business community. They organized a series of networking events, pitching their services to companies looking for opportunities for corporate social responsibility initiatives. This strategy resulted in several new collaborations, providing CSN with a diversified source of funding and enhanced resources. One company, impressed by CSN's commitment to helping unemployed individuals, offered to provide job training facilities and resources, significantly enhancing CSN's job training programs.

Alongside these operational changes, CSN invested significantly in improving internal communication and staff morale. Regular staff meetings, town halls, and open dialogues were instituted to keep employees informed about the organization's progress and to address their concerns and anxieties. The leadership team actively sought feedback from staff, integrating their suggestions into the evolving crisis response strategy. This transparent approach helped to foster a sense of shared purpose and collective resilience, improving staff morale and improving overall organizational cohesiveness. This also led to a reduction in employee turnover, preserving valuable institutional knowledge and expertise.

Furthermore, CSN engaged in extensive community outreach initiatives to rebuild trust and confidence among the population they served. They organized community forums, town hall meetings, and regular updates to communicate their crisis response strategy, highlight the impact of funding reductions, and emphasize the organization's continued dedication to community welfare. These efforts not only helped to improve public perception but also fostered greater community engagement, resulting in increased volunteer support and community fundraising initiatives.

The outcome of CSN's comprehensive crisis response was remarkable. While the economic downturn posed a serious challenge, CSN not only survived but emerged stronger, with a more diversified funding base, streamlined operations, and enhanced community engagement. The crisis forced CSN to fundamentally re-evaluate its operational model, transitioning from a reliance on government funding to a more resilient and sustainable structure based on diversified funding streams and proactive community engagement. The organization's adaptive leadership approach, characterized by collaboration, transparency, and a commitment to community partnership, proved crucial in navigating the crisis and ultimately enhancing its effectiveness and sustainability.

The case study of CSN provides a powerful illustration of adaptive leadership in the non-profit sector. It showcases the importance of moving beyond reactive crisis management to a more proactive, holistic approach encompassing diversified funding strategies, operational efficiency improvements, and strong community partnerships. The organization's success underscores the critical role of empowered leadership, open communication, and employee engagement in building organizational resilience in the face of significant challenges.

CSN's transformation underscores the potential for non-profit organizations to not only survive but thrive by embracing change, fostering innovation, and adapting to a dynamic environment. The experience of CSN demonstrates that a crisis can be a catalyst for positive transformation, leading to improved efficiency, stronger community ties, and greater organizational resilience. The legacy of this crisis serves as a valuable lesson for other non-profit organizations, emphasizing the importance of proactive planning, adaptable leadership, and a deep understanding of their communities' needs.

Case Study A Small Business Scaling Rapidly

This case study focuses on "InnovateTech," a small software development firm specializing in custom mobile applications. Founded by two recent college graduates, InnovateTech initially operated as a lean, agile team, quickly gaining a reputation for innovative solutions and exceptional client service. Their early success was built on a strong foundation of collaborative teamwork, direct client communication, and a shared passion for technology.

Word-of-mouth referrals fueled their growth, leading to a steady influx of projects and a corresponding expansion of the team. However, this rapid growth presented unforeseen challenges.

The initial organizational structure, designed for a small, close-knit team, proved inadequate for managing a larger workforce. Communication channels became congested, decision-making processes slowed, and the previously efficient workflow became fragmented. The founders, accustomed to hands-on involvement in every aspect of the business, found themselves overwhelmed by administrative tasks, hindering their ability to focus on strategic planning and innovation. The collaborative spirit that characterized the company's early days began to erode, replaced by a sense of isolation and inefficiency. Client satisfaction, previously a key metric, started to decline due to longer project timelines and communication breakdowns.

Recognizing the need for a more structured approach, the founders implemented a phased strategy to address the challenges of rapid scaling. The first phase focused on improving internal communication and collaboration. They introduced project management software, establishing clear roles, responsibilities, and reporting structures. Regular team meetings, initially informal brainstorming sessions, evolved into structured progress reviews, ensuring alignment across projects and teams. The implementation of a company-wide instant messaging system facilitated quicker communication and improved responsiveness to client inquiries.

The second phase centered on refining the company's operational processes. InnovateTech implemented a standardized project lifecycle, breaking down complex projects into smaller, manageable tasks with clearly defined deliverables. This allowed for better tracking of progress, improved resource allocation, and clearer identification of potential bottlenecks. They also adopted agile methodologies, incorporating daily stand-up meetings and sprint reviews to enhance team collaboration and responsiveness to changing client requirements.

The third phase addressed the leadership challenge. The founders, while possessing technical expertise and entrepreneurial drive, lacked formal management experience. They recognized the need for experienced leadership to guide the company through its growth trajectory. They hired a seasoned operations manager with a proven track record of scaling technology companies. This new addition brought valuable insights into organizational structure, operational efficiency, and talent management. The operations manager played a crucial role in mentoring the founders and empowering team leaders, fostering a culture of shared responsibility and leadership development within the organization.

To maintain its core values of innovation and client service amidst rapid growth, InnovateTech established a dedicated customer success team. This team served as a direct point of contact for clients, providing regular updates, addressing concerns, and ensuring a high level of client satisfaction. They proactively sought client feedback, using this information to improve processes and enhance the overall client experience. The customer success team also played a critical role in identifying new opportunities for product development and service enhancement, aligning with the company's commitment to innovation.

InnovateTech invested heavily in employee development and training. They created a comprehensive onboarding program for new hires, equipping them with the necessary skills and knowledge to contribute effectively to the team. They also provided ongoing professional development opportunities, including workshops, conferences, and mentorship programs, encouraging employees to enhance their skills and pursue career advancement within the company. This commitment to employee growth resulted in improved employee retention and a stronger organizational culture.

Another key aspect of InnovateTech's scaling strategy was a focus on financial management. As the company grew, they implemented more sophisticated financial tracking systems to monitor cash flow, expenses, and profitability. They developed a strategic financial plan, identifying key performance indicators (KPIs) and setting realistic growth targets. This ensured that the company remained financially stable and sustainable during its period of rapid expansion. They also developed a clear revenue projection model that helped them secure additional funding when necessary. This strategic planning proved instrumental in navigating the complexities of rapid growth.

The outcome of InnovateTech's focused scaling strategy was remarkable. The company not only survived its rapid growth phase but thrived, achieving significant increases in revenue, market share, and employee satisfaction. Their proactive approach to addressing the challenges of scaling, encompassing enhanced communication, streamlined operations, experienced leadership, and a commitment to employee development, proved instrumental in sustaining the company's core values and ensuring its long-term success. The case study of InnovateTech demonstrates that rapid growth, while presenting significant challenges, can be effectively managed with a strategic and proactive approach, fostering sustainable growth and organizational success. It highlights the importance of adapting organizational structure, improving communication, developing strong leadership, and maintaining a focus on core values.

InnovateTech's success serves as a valuable example for other small businesses seeking to scale up effectively. It reinforces the idea that strategic planning, coupled with adaptable leadership and a commitment to employee development, are essential for navigating the complexities of rapid growth and achieving sustained success. The company's experience underscores the importance of proactive planning, organizational agility, and a culture that values both innovation and employee well-being.

The InnovateTech case study also provides valuable insights into the critical role of continuous learning and adaptation. Throughout its growth journey, the company demonstrated a willingness to embrace new technologies, refine its processes, and adapt its leadership style to meet the evolving needs of the business. This flexibility and adaptability were instrumental in overcoming challenges and achieving significant success. The company's willingness to experiment with different strategies and adjust its approach based on results underscores the importance of continuous improvement and learning in the context of rapid growth.

InnovateTech's success can be attributed to its ability to maintain a strong focus on its core values even as it scaled. The company's commitment to innovation, client service, and employee development remained central to its strategy throughout its growth journey. This emphasis on core values helped to build a strong organizational culture that attracted and retained top talent, fostering a sense of purpose and shared commitment among employees. Maintaining this core identity during a period of rapid growth prevented a loss of the company's original spirit and ensured the continued loyalty of both employees and clients.

Finally, the InnovateTech case study demonstrates the importance of proactively seeking external expertise. The decision to hire a seasoned operations manager played a pivotal role in the company's successful scaling. This external perspective provided valuable insights and guidance, helping the founders to navigate the complexities of rapid growth and avoid common pitfalls. The willingness to seek external support highlights the importance of recognizing limitations and proactively addressing them to ensure continued success. The experience of InnovateTech demonstrates that seeking external expertise is not a sign of weakness but a strategic investment in long-term growth and stability. This proactive approach to seeking guidance and support helped to ensure that InnovateTech was well-equipped to handle the challenges associated with rapid growth. The successful scaling of InnovateTech serves as a powerful example of how effective leadership, coupled with a strategic and adaptable approach, can transform a small business into a thriving organization.

Cross Case Analysis and Synthesis of Key Learnings

This chapter has explored adaptive leadership through four distinct case studies, each presenting unique challenges and opportunities within diverse organizational settings. Now, we move to a cross-case analysis, synthesizing the key learnings to extract actionable insights applicable across a broader spectrum of organizations facing periods of significant change. This comparative approach allows us to identify common threads of successful adaptation, highlight contrasting strategies, and ultimately build a more robust understanding of what constitutes effective adaptive leadership.

A primary commonality across all four case studies is the crucial role of proactive anticipation and strategic foresight. While each organization faced unforeseen challenges – whether rapid growth, market disruption, or technological advancement – those that demonstrated a higher degree of foresight and proactive planning tended to navigate these turbulent waters more successfully. InnovateTech, for example, despite its rapid growth, proactively implemented structured processes and leadership development initiatives to mitigate potential problems before they escalated into crises. Similarly, Precision Manufacturing, by anticipating the shift in consumer preferences, was able to reposition its product offerings and maintain its market share. This proactive approach underscores the importance of continuously monitoring the external environment, identifying potential threats and opportunities, and developing contingency plans to address emerging challenges. In essence, the organizations that thrived were not simply reactive; they were proactive, anticipating change and preparing for various eventualities.

Another recurring theme is the critical importance of effective communication and collaboration. In all the case studies, open and transparent communication played a pivotal role in facilitating adaptation. Organizations that fostered a culture of open dialogue, active listening, and shared decision-making were better equipped to adapt to change. Conversely, organizations where communication was fragmented or siloed often struggled to respond effectively. This highlights the need for leaders to create communication channels that facilitate the rapid dissemination of information, foster collaboration across different departments and levels of the organization, and ensure that all stakeholders have a voice in the decision-making process. Specifically, the implementation of clear and consistent communication protocols, regular feedback mechanisms, and inclusive decision-making processes emerged as essential elements in the success of adaptive leadership.

The ability to build and leverage organizational resilience also stands out as a key success factor. Resilience, in this context, isn't simply the capacity to withstand shocks; it's the capacity to learn from those shocks and adapt accordingly. Organizations that possessed a strong foundation of shared values, a culture of learning, and a commitment to continuous improvement were better equipped to navigate turbulent periods. CSN for instance, successfully navigated a significant economic downturn by leveraging its flexible organizational structure and strong employee engagement to adapt to reduced resource levels. This resilience was not merely a passive characteristic; it was actively cultivated through leadership commitment to employee development and a culture that promoted experimentation and learning from failure. The case studies highlight that resilience isn't simply a trait inherent in an organization; it's a cultivated capability requiring a structured approach.

The case studies reveal the critical role of leadership in driving adaptation. However, the nature of effective leadership during periods of change differs significantly from traditional management styles. In all the successful examples, leaders demonstrated a commitment to empowering their teams, fostering collaboration, and promoting a shared sense of purpose. They were not merely managers controlling resources, but rather facilitators, guiding and supporting their teams through the adaptation process. They encouraged experimentation, embraced innovation, and provided their teams with the necessary tools and resources to navigate uncertainty. This underscores a shift away from traditional command-and-control leadership towards a more collaborative and empowering approach.

Successful leaders fostered a climate of trust and psychological safety, encouraging open communication and constructive feedback. They facilitated shared understanding of the challenges faced and involved their teams in the problem-solving process, leading to greater ownership and commitment to the adaptation efforts. They were adept at adjusting their leadership styles to meet the evolving needs of the organization, embodying adaptability themselves.

Interestingly, there are notable differences in the approaches adopted by the organizations studied. While one organization successfully navigated change through a top-down, centralized approach, emphasizing strategic planning and decisive leadership, another employed a more decentralized, bottom-up approach, empowering employees to adapt at the operational level.

These varied approaches highlight the absence of a one-size-fits-all solution in adaptive leadership. The optimal approach depends heavily on the specific context of the organization, its culture, its industry, and the nature of the changes faced. However, despite the differences in their approaches, all the successful organizations shared a common thread: a clear understanding of their core values and a strong commitment to maintaining those values even amidst significant change.

This commitment to core values served as a compass, guiding decisions and ensuring alignment during periods of uncertainty and adaptation. The synthesis of these case studies offers valuable insights into building a robust organizational capacity for adaptation. Key lessons learned emphasize the proactive nature of effective adaptation, the pivotal role of communication and collaboration, the importance of fostering organizational resilience, and the need for adaptive leadership styles. A holistic approach, encompassing anticipation, open communication, resilience building, and empowering leadership, emerges as the foundation for navigating change successfully. Further, the diverse approaches highlight the importance of understanding the specific context and adopting strategies tailored to the organization's unique needs. The ability to learn, adapt, and evolve is not simply a desirable trait; it's a necessity for survival and flourishing in today's dynamic environment.

The success stories highlighted within these case studies should not be interpreted as simplistic replications. Each organization's journey was unique, shaped by its specific circumstances, industry dynamics, and internal culture. However, by identifying recurring themes and common practices, we can develop a deeper understanding of the fundamental principles that underpin adaptive leadership. This understanding empowers organizations to develop their own strategies for navigating change, leveraging the insights gained from other organizations' experiences while acknowledging the need to adapt those insights to their own unique context.

Beyond the individual case studies, this cross-analysis offers a framework for a continuous learning process. By critically examining different approaches, organizations can identify best practices and adapt them to their specific situations. This reflective process fosters a culture of learning and improvement, allowing organizations to constantly refine their adaptive capabilities. Adaptive leadership is not a destination but a journey, requiring continuous learning, evaluation, and refinement based on ongoing experiences and emerging challenges. The ability to continuously learn and adapt will be the defining characteristic of successful organizations in the future.

Finally, the findings of this cross-case analysis underscore the significant role of leadership development in fostering adaptability. Leaders must be equipped with the skills and competencies necessary to navigate change effectively. This includes not only developing strategic foresight and decision-making abilities but also fostering a culture of open communication, collaboration, and learning. Investing in leadership development programs that focus on adaptive leadership principles is therefore crucial for ensuring organizational resilience and successful adaptation in the face of unforeseen challenges. Organizations must prioritize leadership training that cultivates agility, empowers others, promotes a growth mindset, and encourages continuous learning. This investment in leadership capability will yield significant returns in terms of organizational adaptability and overall success. The insights gathered from this cross-case analysis serve as a guide for leaders seeking to cultivate a culture of adaptive leadership within their organizations, enabling them to effectively navigate the complexities of change and emerge stronger and more resilient in the process.

Chapter 9: Developing Your Adaptive Leadership Journey

Creating a Personalized Development Plan

Building upon the insights gleaned from our cross-case analysis of adaptive leadership, we now turn our attention to a crucial next step: the development of a personalized plan for enhancing your own adaptive leadership capabilities. The previous chapters have provided a theoretical framework and practical examples; this section empowers you to translate that knowledge into concrete action, fostering your own journey of continuous growth and improvement.

The process of developing an effective personalized development plan begins with a thorough self-assessment. This isn't merely a superficial exercise; it's a deep dive into your strengths, weaknesses, and areas for growth within the context of adaptive leadership. Consider the key attributes we've explored: proactive anticipation, effective communication, fostering resilience, and employing empowering leadership styles. For each of these, honestly evaluate your current proficiency. Where do you excel? Where do you need improvement? Be brutally honest with yourself; self-awareness is the cornerstone of personal development.

To facilitate this self-assessment, consider using a structured approach. You might employ a SWOT analysis – identifying your Strengths, Weaknesses, Opportunities, and Threats. In the context of adaptive leadership, your strengths might include exceptional communication skills, a proven track record of navigating complex situations, or a natural ability to build consensus. Your weaknesses might be a tendency towards micromanagement, a reluctance to delegate, or difficulty embracing uncertainty. Opportunities might include access to leadership development programs, mentoring opportunities, or exposure to diverse perspectives. Threats might be resistance to change within your organization, limited resources, or a lack of support from senior management.

Beyond the SWOT analysis, consider engaging in self-reflection exercises. Think back to specific instances where you demonstrated adaptive leadership skills – what worked well? What could have been improved? Similarly, reflect on situations where you struggled to adapt – what were the contributing factors? What lessons did you learn? Journaling can be a powerful tool for this process, allowing you to capture your thoughts and insights in a structured manner. This reflective process is crucial; it transforms passive learning into active engagement, anchoring your understanding in your own lived experiences.

Once you've completed your self-assessment, the next step is to identify specific, measurable, achievable, relevant, and time-bound (SMART) goals. Vague aspirations are unhelpful; you need concrete targets that will guide your development efforts. For instance, instead of aiming to "improve communication skills," set a SMART goal such as: "Increase the frequency of team meetings from once a week to twice a week to facilitate more open and frequent communication, by the end of the quarter." This provides a clear measure of progress and a timeframe for achievement. Setting SMART goals for each identified area of weakness is critical. If your self-assessment revealed a weakness is proactive anticipation, a SMART goal might be: "Implement a weekly environmental scanning process, identifying potential threats and opportunities related to [specific area], within the next month." Or, if your weakness lies in fostering resilience, a SMART goal could be: "Attend a workshop on building organizational resilience and implement one new strategy within my team based on the workshop learnings, before the end of the year." These specific goals provide concrete steps towards your overarching aim of becoming a more effective adaptive leader.

Creating a detailed action plan is the next essential step. Your action plan should outline the specific steps you'll take to achieve your SMART goals. For each goal, break it down into smaller, manageable tasks. For example, if your goal is to improve your communication skills, your action plan might include attending a communication workshop, practicing active listening techniques during team meetings, and seeking feedback from colleagues on your communication style. Assign realistic timelines to each task and ensure that your plan is both comprehensive and achievable. Flexibility is key; be prepared to adjust your plan as circumstances change.

Throughout this development process, remember the power of seeking feedback from others. Solicit feedback from your colleagues, superiors, and subordinates, seeking constructive criticism on your leadership style and areas for improvement. Feedback provides invaluable external perspectives, often illuminating blind spots in your self-perception. Encourage open and honest communication, creating a safe space for feedback and ensuring that it is delivered in a constructive and supportive manner. Consider implementing regular 360-degree feedback processes, incorporating perspectives from various stakeholders to gain a holistic view of your strengths and weaknesses.

Finally, cultivate a support network to assist in your development journey. This might include mentors, coaches, or trusted colleagues who can provide guidance, support, and encouragement. Mentors can offer valuable insights and advice based on their own experiences, while coaches can provide structured support and accountability, helping you stay on track and overcome obstacles. A strong support network is crucial for navigating the challenges of personal and professional growth, providing a vital source of encouragement and perspective during difficult times. Regular check-ins with your mentors and coaches provide valuable opportunities to reflect on progress, adjust your strategies, and celebrate successes along the way.

Creating and implementing a personalized development plan is not a one-time event, but an ongoing process of continuous learning and improvement. Regularly review and update your plan, adapting it to reflect your progress, changing circumstances, and emerging challenges. The journey towards becoming a more effective adaptive leader is a lifelong endeavor, requiring constant self-reflection, continuous learning, and a commitment to personal and professional growth. Remember that setbacks are inevitable, but they offer valuable opportunities for learning and growth. Embrace them as part of the journey, analyzing what went wrong, adjusting your approach, and moving forward with renewed determination. By embracing this iterative approach, you can cultivate a culture of continuous improvement, both in your own leadership journey and within your organization. The ultimate goal is not simply to acquire new skills but to fundamentally transform your leadership approach, building a foundation for agility, resilience, and success in the face of any challenge. Your personalized development plan is your roadmap for that transformative journey.

Building Your Adaptive Leadership Network

Building a robust and supportive network is paramount to your success in cultivating adaptive leadership. This isn't simply about collecting business cards; it's about cultivating genuine relationships with individuals who can offer diverse perspectives, challenge your assumptions, and provide unwavering support during times of uncertainty. Your network should be a diverse ecosystem, composed of individuals who complement your skills and experiences, offering a variety of viewpoints and expertise. Think of it as a board of advisors for your leadership journey, constantly providing feedback and insights that enhance your adaptability.

The first step in building your adaptive leadership network involves identifying potential mentors and allies. These individuals don't need to be formally designated as mentors; they can be colleagues, supervisors, industry experts, or even individuals you've met through professional development programs. Look for people who demonstrate the adaptive leadership qualities you aspire to, possess strong communication and interpersonal skills, and are willing to share their knowledge and experience. Consider those who have successfully navigated complex challenges,
demonstrating resilience and strategic thinking in the face of adversity. Their lived experiences provide invaluable lessons you can learn from, far beyond the scope of textbooks or theoretical models.

When selecting potential mentors, consider their areas of expertise. Do they have experience in areas where you need improvement? Do they have a track record of success in similar situations to those you anticipate facing? Seek out individuals with complementary skills and perspectives; a diverse network offers a broader range of insights and challenges your own assumptions. Avoid individuals who are simply "yes-men" or those who lack the courage to provide constructive criticism. You need individuals who will provide honest, even if sometimes difficult, feedback to accelerate your growth.

Once you've identified potential mentors and allies, the next step involves building genuine relationships. This isn't a transactional process; it's about establishing trust and mutual respect. Begin by initiating contact, perhaps by requesting a brief informational interview or simply expressing your interest in learning from their experience. Prepare thoughtful questions that demonstrate your genuine interest and willingness to learn. Listen actively during your conversations, demonstrating respect for their time and expertise. Follow up after your conversations with a thank-you note, reinforcing your interest in building a lasting relationship.

Beyond formal mentorship, cultivate relationships with peers and colleagues across your organization and industry. Participate in professional development programs, attend industry events, and engage in online communities to expand your network. Seek out individuals with different backgrounds and perspectives, as these individuals will challenge your assumptions and broaden your understanding of leadership challenges. These peer-to-peer relationships offer valuable opportunities for informal learning, providing a sense of community and mutual support. Regular interaction, even informal coffee chats or lunch meetings, will nurture these relationships, fostering a sense of collaboration and shared purpose.

Effective networking isn't about self-promotion; it's about building genuine connections. Focus on creating value for others in your network, offering support and assistance whenever possible. This reciprocal approach fosters long-term, mutually beneficial relationships. Be proactive in offering help to others; this reinforces your commitment to collaboration and creates goodwill. When you provide value to others, they are more likely to reciprocate, fostering a strong and mutually supportive network. Remember, networking is a two-way street; you receive as much as you give.

Leveraging your network effectively requires conscious effort. Regularly communicate with your contacts, sharing updates on your progress and seeking their input on challenges you face. Don't hesitate to ask for advice or guidance when you need it; your network is there to support you. When seeking advice, be specific about the challenge you face, providing context and outlining the options you've considered. This will facilitate more informed and helpful feedback. Remember to acknowledge the time and expertise of your network members, demonstrating your appreciation for their support.

Maintaining your network requires ongoing effort. Stay in touch with your contacts, even when you don't need immediate assistance. This reinforces relationships and strengthens the bonds within your network. Regularly participate in industry events and professional development programs to expand your network and stay abreast of current trends. Utilize online platforms like LinkedIn to connect with individuals in your field, participating in discussions and sharing relevant content. This keeps your network active and relevant, ensuring that it remains a valuable resource throughout your leadership journey.

To further enhance your networking strategy, consider implementing structured approaches. Maintain a detailed contact list, noting key interactions and areas of expertise for each individual in your network. Regularly review your network, identifying potential gaps or areas where additional connections would be beneficial. This structured approach enables you to maximize the value of your network, ensuring that you have access to the expertise you need when you need it. Moreover, periodically reflect on your network's effectiveness; are you receiving the support you need? Are you actively contributing to its strength? This reflective process ensures continuous improvement and optimization of your network.

Building your adaptive leadership network isn't a passive process; it's an active, ongoing endeavor requiring continuous cultivation. Regularly assess your network's effectiveness, identifying areas for growth and seeking opportunities to strengthen existing connections. Don't be afraid to reach out to people outside your immediate circle, expanding your network beyond your comfort zone. The more diverse your network, the more adaptable and resilient you'll become as a leader. Remember, building a strong network is not just about who you know, but about the relationships you cultivate and the value you create for others. By consistently nurturing these relationships, you create a powerful support system that empowers your adaptive leadership journey and enhances your ability to navigate the complexities of the modern world.

Consider the value of reciprocal mentorship. While you benefit greatly from the insights and experience of your mentors, also consider how you can contribute to the growth and development of others. This reciprocal approach strengthens relationships and fosters a culture of collaboration and mutual support. Mentoring junior colleagues or sharing your knowledge and experience with others can be incredibly rewarding, enhancing your own leadership skills while also making a positive impact on the development of others. This reciprocal engagement strengthens your network, transforming it from a resource for personal development into a collaborative ecosystem that contributes to the success of your organization as a whole.

Finally, remember that your network is a dynamic entity, constantly evolving as your needs and circumstances change. Be open to new connections, always seeking opportunities to learn and grow. Regularly evaluate the value your network provides, adjusting your approach to maximize its effectiveness. Embrace change and be prepared to adapt your networking strategies as your career and leadership journey progress. The strength of your adaptive leadership network directly impacts your ability to navigate challenges, make informed decisions, and achieve lasting success. It's an investment that pays dividends throughout your entire career. By strategically building and nurturing this vital resource, you position yourself for a future of confident, effective, and adaptive leadership.

Seeking Mentorship and Continuous Feedback

Seeking mentorship and continuous feedback is not merely an optional add-on to your adaptive leadership journey; it's a cornerstone of sustainable growth and effectiveness. In a world characterized by constant change and unprecedented complexity, relying solely on your own experiences and instincts is insufficient. A robust system of mentorship and feedback provides the crucial external perspective and validation needed to navigate ambiguity and adapt effectively.

The first crucial step is identifying potential mentors. This process requires careful consideration and self-reflection. Start by identifying your specific leadership weaknesses and areas for improvement. Where do you feel your skills are lacking? What types of challenges consistently stump you? Understanding these vulnerabilities allows you to target mentors who possess the complementary expertise and experience necessary to address these gaps. Don't limit your search to individuals within your immediate organization. Explore your professional network, industry events, conferences, and even online platforms to uncover individuals with relevant experience and a willingness to mentor. Look for mentors who not only possess technical expertise but also demonstrate strong emotional intelligence, empathy, and a commitment to fostering the growth of others.

Once you've identified potential candidates, approach them with humility and respect. Prepare a concise and compelling rationale for why you've chosen them as a potential mentor. Clearly articulate your goals and aspirations, emphasizing your commitment to self-improvement and your willingness to actively participate in the mentorship relationship. Remember, mentorship is a two-way street; it requires active engagement and mutual benefit. Your request should demonstrate that you understand this dynamic and are prepared to invest the necessary time and effort. A well-crafted email or introductory letter expressing your admiration for their work and highlighting specific aspects of their expertise that resonate with your goals can be an effective starting point.

Effective communication is crucial throughout the mentorship relationship. Regularly schedule meetings, setting clear agendas to ensure productive discussions. Be prepared to actively listen, asking thoughtful questions to delve deeper into your mentor's insights and experiences. Avoid monopolizing the conversation; instead, create space for open dialogue and mutual exchange of ideas. Maintain meticulous notes from each meeting, documenting key insights and action items. This will help ensure that you can revisit and apply their advice effectively. And remember to show gratitude; express your appreciation for their time, expertise, and guidance. A simple thank you note or a thoughtful gift can go a long way in solidifying the relationship.

Beyond formal mentorship, cultivate a culture of continuous feedback within your professional sphere. Actively seek feedback from colleagues, subordinates, and supervisors. Regularly solicit 360-degree reviews to gain a comprehensive understanding of your leadership strengths and weaknesses from multiple perspectives. Don't limit your feedback sources to only positive reviews; actively seek out constructive criticism, as this is often where the most significant opportunities for improvement lie. When receiving feedback, resist the urge to become defensive or dismissive. Instead, listen attentively, asking clarifying questions to ensure a full understanding of the feedback given. Show your willingness to learn and grow and avoid interrupting the feedback provider. This receptive attitude is crucial for maximizing the value of the feedback received.

Processing and acting on feedback requires a structured approach. After receiving feedback, take some time to reflect on the comments. Identify recurring themes or patterns that emerge across multiple sources. Prioritize areas for immediate improvement, focusing on those that directly impact your effectiveness as a leader. Develop a concrete plan of action, setting specific, measurable, achievable, relevant, and time-bound (SMART) goals to address these areas for improvement. Regularly review your progress, adapting your approach as needed based on your experiences and ongoing feedback. Don't be afraid to seek clarification or further explanation if you are unsure how to interpret or implement the feedback.

Also, consider incorporating formal feedback mechanisms into your leadership style. Regular one-on-one meetings with team members provide opportunities for both upward and downward feedback, fostering open communication and mutual growth. Implement anonymous feedback surveys to gather candid insights from those who might be hesitant to provide direct criticism. Make sure to communicate to your team that you value constructive feedback and are actively seeking ways to improve your leadership style. Make it clear that you intend to use this feedback to create a more effective and supportive workplace for everyone. Remember, continuous feedback is not just about addressing weaknesses; it also provides valuable opportunities to identify and build upon existing strengths. Leverage positive feedback to reinforce effective leadership behaviors and expand on your areas of excellence. Seek out opportunities to showcase and develop your strengths. Celebrate successes and actively learn from both triumphs and setbacks. View feedback, both positive and negative, as opportunities for growth and development. This positive mindset transforms the feedback process into a powerful catalyst for ongoing improvement and enhances your capacity for adaptive leadership.

Building resilience is inextricably linked to the pursuit of mentorship and feedback. Seeking mentorship provides a supportive environment where you can share challenges and vulnerabilities without fear of judgment. Constructive feedback offers insights and strategies to effectively overcome obstacles and learn from mistakes. This continuous process of learning and adapting fosters resilience, empowering you to navigate setbacks with greater confidence and equanimity. Regular self-reflection, informed by feedback from mentors and colleagues, enhances your capacity to recognize patterns of resilience and develop coping mechanisms to deal with stress and adversity.

Finally, recognize that the journey of adaptive leadership, fueled by mentorship and feedback, is a continuous process. It is not a destination but a lifelong endeavor that requires ongoing commitment and self-reflection. Embrace the opportunities for growth and development that come with seeking mentorship and actively soliciting feedback. By actively cultivating a culture of feedback within your organization and building strong mentoring relationships, you empower yourself and your team to navigate the complexities of the modern world with confidence, resilience, and unwavering effectiveness. Remember that continuous improvement is not merely a leadership aspiration; it's a necessity in today's rapidly changing environment.

Embracing Lifelong Learning and Continuous Improvement

Embracing lifelong learning isn't merely a suggestion for the adaptive leader; it's a fundamental requirement. The landscape of business, technology, and societal norms shifts with breathtaking speed. Leaders who cling to outdated knowledge and skill sets are destined to be left behind, their organizations struggling to keep pace with the relentless tide of change. Adaptive leadership demands a commitment to continuous growth, a thirst for new knowledge, and a willingness to embrace unfamiliar territory. This section explores practical strategies for staying current, expanding your knowledge base, and cultivating a culture of continuous improvement within your organization.

One of the most effective methods for staying current is actively engaging with industry trends. This isn't about passively absorbing information; it's about actively seeking it out, analyzing it, and applying its implications to your leadership style and organizational strategy. Subscribe to relevant industry publications, both print and digital. Attend conferences and workshops focused on your sector, actively participating in discussions and networking with peers. Engage with thought leaders and influencers on social media platforms, critically evaluating their insights and perspectives. The goal is not to simply consume information, but to actively process it, identifying opportunities for innovation and improvement within your own context. This active engagement transforms passive observation into proactive adaptation.

Beyond industry-specific knowledge, broadening your intellectual horizons is crucial. Adaptive leadership necessitates a flexible and versatile mind, capable of drawing insights from diverse fields and perspectives.

Explore topics outside your immediate area of expertise. Read books and articles on history, psychology, sociology, and the arts. Attend lectures and seminars that challenge your assumptions and broaden your understanding of the world.

Consider exploring fields seemingly unrelated to your current role—the surprising connections and unexpected insights gleaned from such explorations often prove invaluable in developing creative solutions to complex problems. This intellectual curiosity fuels innovation and enhances your ability to see the big picture, fostering adaptability in the face of unexpected challenges.

Formal learning opportunities also play a vital role in the adaptive leader's journey. Online courses offer a flexible and accessible avenue for expanding your knowledge and skill set. Platforms like Coursera, edX, and LinkedIn Learning provide a wealth of courses on a vast range of topics, from project management and data analysis to emotional intelligence and leadership development. These platforms allow you to tailor your learning to your specific needs and interests, focusing on areas where you seek improvement or wish to gain new skills. Consider dedicating a specific amount of time each week to focused learning, treating it as a non-negotiable part of your professional development. This commitment demonstrates your dedication to continuous growth and sets a positive example for your team.

Leverage the power of mentorship and coaching. A skilled mentor can provide invaluable guidance and support as you navigate the complexities of leadership. They can offer personalized feedback, challenge your assumptions, and provide fresh perspectives on your challenges. A coach can help you develop specific skills and strategies for enhancing your leadership effectiveness. These relationships provide invaluable support and accelerate your learning process, ensuring your development remains focused and productive. Consider investing in professional coaching to accelerate your growth in specific areas.

Beyond formal learning, self-directed learning holds immense power. Identify your personal learning style and tailor your approach accordingly. Some individuals thrive in structured environments, benefiting from formal courses and workshops. Others prefer a more independent approach, diving into books, articles, and podcasts at their own pace. Regardless of your preferred method, the key is to actively engage in the learning process, critically evaluating information and applying it to your leadership style. Maintain a learning journal, documenting key insights, challenges, and successes. This record serves as a valuable resource, allowing you to track your progress and reflect on your learning journey.

However, knowledge without application is sterile. The adaptive leader actively seeks opportunities to put their learning into practice. This could involve leading a new project, taking on a challenging assignment, or mentoring junior colleagues. These practical experiences solidify your learning and allow you to test your newly acquired skills in real-world scenarios. Embrace challenges as opportunities for growth, viewing setbacks as valuable learning experiences. Actively seek feedback on your performance, both positive and constructive, using it to refine your approach and continuously improve. This iterative process of learning, application, and feedback is crucial for fostering genuine growth.

The concept of a "growth mindset" is central to lifelong learning. Individuals with a growth mindset view challenges as opportunities for learning and development, not as threats to their self-worth. They embrace failure as a valuable learning experience, viewing it as a stepping stone towards improvement rather than an indication of incompetence. They believe that their abilities and intelligence are malleable, capable of being developed and enhanced through dedication and effort. Cultivating a growth mindset is essential for the adaptive leader, enabling them to navigate uncertainty and change with confidence and resilience. This mindset transforms obstacles into opportunities, fostering a culture of continuous improvement within the organization.

This requires a conscious shift in thinking. Leaders must move away from a fixed mindset—where abilities are seen as inherent and unchangeable to a growth mindset—where abilities are seen as malleable and capable of improvement. This involves challenging negative self-talk, embracing constructive criticism, and celebrating both individual and team successes. A growth mindset fosters a culture of continuous learning and improvement, where mistakes are seen as learning opportunities, and experimentation is encouraged. The leader who embodies a growth mindset inspires similar attitudes in their team, creating a dynamic and adaptable organization.

Finally, creating a culture of continuous improvement within your organization is crucial. Leaders need to model the behavior they expect from their team members, actively demonstrating a commitment to lifelong learning and continuous growth. This involves investing in training and development programs, encouraging employees to pursue further education and professional development opportunities, and creating a supportive environment where learning and experimentation are valued. Regularly solicit feedback from employees, seeking their perspectives on how the organization can improve its processes and outcomes. This fosters a sense of shared ownership and responsibility for continuous improvement, leading to a more dynamic and innovative organization.

The journey of adaptive leadership is not a sprint; it's a marathon. It requires unwavering commitment to lifelong learning and continuous improvement. By embracing the strategies discussed above—actively engaging with industry trends, broadening intellectual horizons, leveraging formal and self-directed learning opportunities, and cultivating a growth mindset—leaders can equip themselves and their organizations to navigate the complexities of the modern world with confidence, resilience, and unwavering success. The adaptive leader is not just a manager of tasks, but a lifelong learner, constantly evolving and adapting to the ever-changing demands of the modern business environment. This commitment to continuous growth is not simply an advantage; it's a necessity for survival and success.

Sustaining Your Adaptive Leadership Practice

Sustaining your adaptive leadership practice demands a commitment that extends far beyond the initial adoption of new skills and strategies. It requires a conscious and ongoing effort to cultivate a resilient mindset, continually refine your leadership capabilities, and adapt to the ever-shifting landscape of the modern business world. This isn't simply about reacting to change; it's about proactively shaping your response and ensuring your leadership remains effective and relevant in the long term.

One of the cornerstones of sustaining adaptive leadership is self-reflection. Regular introspection is critical to identifying areas for improvement, recognizing personal biases, and evaluating the effectiveness of your leadership style. This isn't about self-criticism; it's about honest self-assessment. Schedule dedicated time for reflection, perhaps using a journal or a quiet space for contemplation. Consider using frameworks such as SWOT analysis to assess your strengths, weaknesses, opportunities, and threats. Reflect on your recent interactions, decisions, and outcomes. What worked well? What could have been improved? What lessons can be learned for future situations?

Regularly soliciting feedback from your team is another crucial component of self-reflection. Create a safe and open environment where team members feel comfortable sharing their honest opinions and perspectives. This feedback, whether positive or constructive, offers valuable insights into your leadership style and its impact on the team. Implement a system for gathering feedback, such as anonymous surveys, one-on-one meetings, or 360-degree feedback assessments. Actively listen to the feedback you receive, regardless of whether it aligns with your own self-perception. Use this feedback to refine your approach and make necessary adjustments to your leadership style. Remember, the goal is continuous improvement, not perfection.

Beyond self-reflection, continuous learning is vital for sustaining an adaptive leadership practice. The world is constantly changing, and so too must your leadership approach. Maintain your commitment to lifelong learning by staying abreast of industry trends, exploring new technologies, and expanding your knowledge base. Continue to engage with industry publications, attend conferences and workshops, and seek out mentorship opportunities. Consider diversifying your learning sources, exploring different formats such as podcasts, online courses, and books. The key is to maintain a consistent commitment to learning and development, ensuring you remain adaptable and relevant in the face of change.

Developing resilience is crucial for sustaining your adaptive leadership journey. Resilience is the ability to bounce back from setbacks and adversity. In the ever-changing landscape of business, setbacks are inevitable. However, it's your response to these setbacks that determines your success. Cultivating resilience involves developing emotional intelligence, fostering a positive mindset, and building strong support networks. Practice mindfulness and stress-management techniques to equip yourself to navigate challenging situations with calm and clarity. Remember, setbacks are opportunities for learning and growth; they are not signs of failure.

Maintaining a growth mindset is another critical aspect of sustaining adaptive leadership. A growth mindset views challenges as opportunities for learning and development, not as threats to self-worth. Individuals with a growth mindset embrace failure as a valuable learning experience, viewing it as a steppingstone towards improvement rather than an indication of incompetence. This mindset fosters a culture of continuous improvement, where experimentation and innovation are encouraged, and mistakes are viewed as learning opportunities. By actively cultivating a growth mindset, you create an environment where your team members feel empowered to take risks, learn from their mistakes, and continuously improve their skills and capabilities.

Adapting to evolving circumstances is essential for long-term success in adaptive leadership. The ability to flexibly adjust your approach and strategies is paramount. This requires a high degree of self-awareness and a willingness to change course when necessary. Regularly assess the effectiveness of your leadership approach, considering the impact of internal and external factors. Are your strategies still aligned with the organization's goals? Are you effectively meeting the needs of your team and the organization? If not, be prepared to make adjustments and adapt your approach as needed. This flexibility ensures you remain relevant and effective in the face of ongoing change.

Sustaining your adaptive leadership practice also involves creating a culture of continuous improvement within your organization. This means fostering a shared commitment to learning, development, and adaptation. Encourage your team to actively participate in learning opportunities, providing them with access to resources, training, and mentorship programs. Create a safe and supportive environment where experimentation is encouraged and mistakes are viewed as valuable learning experiences. Implement systems for gathering feedback from your team, seeking their input on processes, procedures, and strategic decisions. This collaborative approach fosters a shared sense of ownership and responsibility for continuous improvement.

Finally, maintaining your motivation is essential for sustaining your adaptive leadership practice over the long term. This requires a deep-seated commitment to personal and professional growth, as well as a strong sense of purpose and meaning in your work. Find ways to stay inspired and motivated, engaging in activities that energize and revitalize you. This could include pursuing hobbies, spending time with loved ones, or engaging in activities that promote personal well-being. Remember, leadership is a marathon, not a sprint, and sustaining your practice requires consistent effort and self-care.

In conclusion, sustaining your adaptive leadership practice is a continuous journey that requires ongoing self-reflection, continuous learning, resilience, a growth mindset, and adaptability. By consistently implementing these strategies, you can equip yourself and your organization to navigate the complexities of the modern world, ensuring your leadership remains effective, relevant, and impactful in the long term.

The commitment to ongoing improvement is not just an advantage but a necessity for sustained success in today's dynamic environment. It's about embracing the journey, viewing challenges as opportunities, and cultivating a culture of continuous learning and adaptation within your organization. This approach will ensure that your leadership remains not only relevant but also a source of strength and guidance for years to come. The adaptive leader is a lifelong learner, constantly evolving and adapting to the ever-changing demands of the modern business environment. This commitment to continuous growth is the key to both survival and sustained success.

Acknowledgments

First and foremost, I extend my deepest gratitude to my family and friends for their unwavering support and patience throughout the writing process. Their encouragement and understanding were invaluable, particularly during the challenging moments of research and revision. I am especially indebted to those whose insightful feedback and meticulous editing significantly improved the clarity and impact of this book.

Finally, I acknowledge the countless individuals whose leadership journeys inspired the creation of this work. Their stories of resilience, adaptability, and success serve as powerful reminders of the transformative power of adaptive leadership.

Appendix

This appendix contains supplementary materials to enhance your understanding and application of the concepts presented in *The Leadership Pivot.*

Appendix A: Adaptive Leadership Assessment:

Instructions: Rate yourself on a scale of 1 to 5 for each statement, where 1 means "strongly disagree" and 5 means "strongly agree."

Understanding and Awareness

I am aware of the challenges and uncertainties facing my organization.

I continuously seek feedback to understand my strengths and areas for improvement.

I understand the importance of adaptability in leadership.

Emotional Intelligence

I can manage my emotions effectively, even under stress.

I am empathetic and can understand the emotions and perspectives of others.

I foster a positive and inclusive team environment.

Critical Thinking and Problem-Solving

I approach problems with an open mind and consider multiple perspectives.

I am skilled at identifying the root causes of challenges.

I can generate creative and effective solutions to complex problems.

Change Management

I am comfortable with ambiguity and can navigate through uncertainty.

I effectively communicate changes and their impact to my team.

I can motivate and guide my team through transitions and transformations.

Adaptability and Flexibility

I am open to new ideas and willing to adjust my plans when necessary.

I can quickly adapt to changing circumstances and environments.

I encourage my team to embrace change and continuous improvement.

Strategic Thinking

I have a clear vision for the future and set long-term goals.

I can align my team's efforts with the overall organizational strategy.

I regularly review and adjust strategies based on changing conditions.

Scoring:

Add up your scores for each section.

Reflect on the areas where you scored lower and consider actions you can take to improve in those areas.

Reflection Questions:

What are my strengths as an adaptive leader?

In which areas can I improve my adaptive leadership skills?

What steps can I take to develop my adaptive leadership capabilities further?

Appendix B: Leadership Development Plan

Instructions: Use this template to create your personalized leadership development plan. Reflect on your current leadership capabilities, identify areas for growth, and outline specific actions and timelines to achieve your goals.

Section 1: Self-Assessment

Strengths: Identify your key leadership strengths and how they benefit your team or organization.

Areas for Improvement: Identify areas where you need to develop or improve your leadership skills.

Feedback: Gather feedback from peers, mentors, or team members to gain insight into your leadership style and areas for improvement.

Section 2: Goal Setting

Short-Term Goals (1-6 months): List specific, achievable goals that you aim to accomplish in the short term.

Example: Improve communication skills through active listening and regular feedback sessions.

Medium-Term Goals (6-12 months): List goals that require more time and effort to achieve.

Example: Develop strategic thinking by attending workshops and engaging in strategic planning exercises.

Long-Term Goals (1-3 years): List broader, long-term goals that will significantly impact your leadership journey.

Example: Lead a cross-functional project team to enhance collaboration and innovation within the organization.

Section 3: Strategies and Actions

Training and Development: Identify specific training programs, courses, or workshops that will help you develop the necessary skills to achieve your goals.

Mentorship and Coaching: Seek mentorship or coaching relationships to provide guidance and support in your leadership development.

Practical Experience: Identify opportunities for hands-on leadership experience, such as leading projects, taking on new responsibilities, or participating in leadership programs.

Reading and Research: Compile a list of books, articles, and resources that will enhance your knowledge and understanding of leadership.

Section 4: Timeline and Milestones

Action Plan: Create a detailed action plan with specific steps and timelines for achieving each goal.

Milestones: Set measurable milestones to track your progress and celebrate your achievements along the way.

Review and Adjust: Regularly review your development plan, assess your progress, and adjust as needed to stay on track.

Section 5: Reflection and Evaluation

Self-Reflection: Reflect on your leadership journey, challenges, and accomplishments.

Evaluation: Evaluate the effectiveness of your development plan and identify any areas for improvement.

Next Steps: Outline the next steps in your leadership development journey, including new goals and strategies.

Appendix C: Adaptive Leadership Exercises:

Exercise 1: Identifying Adaptive Challenges

Objective: Learn to distinguish between technical problems and adaptive challenges.

Activity: Ask your team to come up with a list of scenarios and categorize each as a technical problem or an adaptive challenge. Discuss why they categorized them that way and what makes adaptive challenges different from technical problems.

Exercise 2: Stakeholder Mapping

Objective: To understand the perspectives and interests of different stakeholders.

Activity: Create a stakeholder map for a current challenge or project. Identify key stakeholders, their interests, and their potential impact on the situation. Discuss strategies for engaging each stakeholder.

Exercise 3: Reflection on Values

Objective: Reflect on your core values and how they influence your leadership.

Activity: List your top five values and write a brief reflection on how each value impacts your leadership decisions and actions. Highlight any conflicts between values and how to navigate them.

Exercise 4: Adaptive Experimentation

Objective: Promote a culture of experimentation and learning.

Activity: Identify a current challenge and design a small-scale experiment to address it. Outline the hypothesis, steps to implement the experiment, and criteria for success. After conducting the experiment, reflect on the results and lessons learned.

Exercise 5: Emotional Intelligence Journal

Objective: Develop emotional intelligence through regular self-reflection.

Activity: Maintain a daily or weekly journal focused on emotional intelligence. Reflect on situations where emotions played a significant role, how emotions were managed, and what could be done differently in the future.

Exercise 6: Visioning and Strategic Thinking

Objective: Strengthen strategic thinking and visioning capabilities.

Activity: Create a vision statement for your team or organization. Outline long-term goals and the strategies needed to achieve them.

Appendix D: Role-Playing Scenarios

Instructions: Use these role-playing scenarios to practice adaptive leadership skills. Pair up with a partner or work in a group to act out each scenario, focusing on key adaptive leadership principles. After each role-play, debrief and discuss what went well and what could be improved.

Scenario 1: Leading Through Change

Situation: Your organization is undergoing a major restructuring. Some team members are resistant to change and worried about job security.

Objective: Demonstrate effective communication, empathy, and support to guide your team through the transition.

Role-Play: One person plays the leader, and the other plays a concerned team member. Practice addressing concerns, providing reassurance, and outlining the benefits of the change.

Scenario 2: Managing Conflict

Situation: Two team members are in conflict over differing approaches to a project. The tension is affecting team morale and productivity.

Objective: Use conflict resolution skills to mediate the situation and find a collaborative solution.

Role-Play: One person plays the leader, and the others play the conflicting team members. Practice facilitating a constructive conversation, finding common ground, and agreeing on a way forward.

Scenario 3: Encouraging Innovation

Situation: Your team is tasked with developing a new product, but they are stuck in traditional ways of thinking and hesitant to take risks.

Objective: Foster a culture of innovation by encouraging creative thinking and risk-taking.

Role-Play: One person plays the leader, and the others play team members. Practice brainstorming sessions, encouraging out-of-the-box ideas, and creating a safe space for experimentation.

Scenario 4: Navigating Ambiguity

Situation: Your team is working on a project with unclear goals and rapidly changing requirements. Team members are frustrated and unsure how to proceed.

Objective: Demonstrate adaptability and provide clear guidance to navigate the ambiguity.

Role-Play: One person plays the leader, and the others play team members. Practice setting short-term goals, providing regular updates, and adjusting plans as new information emerges.

Scenario 5: Building Trust

Situation: Your team has experienced a recent setback, and trust in leadership is low. Team members are feeling demotivated and disconnected.

Objective: Rebuild trust and foster a positive team environment.

Role-Play: One person plays the leader, and the others play team members. Practice open and honest communication, acknowledging the setbacks, and outlining steps to rebuild trust and move forward.

Debriefing Questions:

How did the leader address the key challenges in each scenario?

What adaptive leadership skills were demonstrated?

What could have been done differently to improve the outcome?

How can these scenarios be applied to real-life situations in your organization?

Glossary

This glossary defines key terms used throughout *The Leadership Pivot*:

Adaptive Leadership:
A leadership approach that emphasizes flexibility, continuous learning, and responsiveness to change.

Resilience:
The ability to bounce back from setbacks and adversity.

Growth Mindset:
A belief that abilities and intelligence can be developed through dedication and hard work.

Emotional Intelligence:
The ability to understand and manage one's own emotions, and the emotions of others.

SWOT Analysis:
A strategic planning technique used to identify Strengths, Weaknesses, Opportunities, and Threats.

360-degree Feedback:
A method of gathering feedback from multiple sources, including superiors, peers, and subordinates.

References

Embrace the Pivot: The Power of Changing Your Mind. Wharton Executive Education.

Book Summary: Pivot by Jenny Blake. Book Summary Club.

Free Leadership Resources from Open Pivot. Open Pivot.

Adaptive Leadership Resources. Adaptive Change Advisors.

Adaptive Leadership: Principles and a Framework for the Future. Atlassian.

Adaptive Leadership Resources. Institute for Conservation Leadership.

Author Biography

Olivia Savage is the author of *The Leadership Pivot* and a seasoned expert in Corporate Learning and Development, with over 20 years of experience driving leadership excellence and transformational change. She has worked with global organizations, including Disney, Nestlé, and Kellanova, specializing in innovative strategies that empower leaders to navigate complexity, inspire teams, and foster sustainable growth.

Olivia is also a thought leader in change management, leveraging AI-powered solutions to help businesses adapt and thrive in an ever-evolving landscape.

www.ingramcontent.com/pod-product-compliance
Lightning Source LLC
Chambersburg PA
CBHW011220120626
46545CB00010B/3083